Race and Hi

Race and Higher Education

Experiences, Challenges and Policy Implications

EDITED BY
TARIQ MODOOD AND TONY ACLAND

POLICY STUDIES INSTITUTE

UNIVERSITY OF WESTMINSTER

PSI is a wholly owned subsidiary of the University of Westminster

© **Policy Studies Institute 1998**

A CIP catalogue record of this book is available from the British Library.

ISBN 0 85374 717 2
PSI Report No. 841

Typeset by Policy Studies Institute
Printed and bound in Great Britain by Athenaeum Press Ltd, Gateshead, Tyne & Wear

Policy Studies Institute is one of Europe's leading research organisations undertaking studies of economic, industrial and social policy and the workings of political institutions. The Institute is a registered charity and is not associated with any political party, pressure group or commercial interest.

For further information contact
Policy Studies Institute, 100 Park Village East, London NW1 3SR
Tel: 0171 468 0468   Fax: 0171 388 0914   Email: pubs@psi.org. uk

Contents

PART THREE
ETHNIC STRATIFICATION IN HIGHER EDUCATION

Figures and Tables

Acronyms and Abbreviations

ADAR	Art and Design Admissions Registry
CRE	Commission for Racial Equality
CVCP	Committee of Vice Chancellors and Principals
DfE	Department for Education
DfEE	Department for Education and Employment
DGH	District General Hospital
GCSE	General Certificate of Secondary Education
GMB	General, Municipal and Boilermakers Union
HE	Higher education
HEFCE	Higher Education Funding Council for England
HEQC	Higher Education Quality Council
HESA	Higher Education Statistics Agency
HNC	Higher National Certificate
ILEA	Inner London Education Authority
NATFHE	National Association of Teachers in Further and Higher Education
OFSTED	Office for Standards in Education
OSCE	Objective Structured Clinical Examination
OSLER	Objective Structured Long Examination Record
PCAS	Polytechnics Central Admissions System
QAA	Quality Assurance Agency
RAE	Research Assessment Exercise
SSM	Special Study Module
UCAS	Universities and Colleges Admissions Service
UCCA	Universities Central Council on Admissions
UEL	University of East London
UNL	University of North London

Contributors

Tony Acland is Head of the Student Development Service at Southampton Institute. He has co-authored a number of community studies, including 'Integration and Segregation Amongst an Asian Community' (*New Community,* 1989), *Changing Ethnicities* (European Sociological Association, Budapest, 1995) and recently *Barriers and Opportunities: The Perceptions of Ethnic Minorities of Southampton SRB* (SRB, 1998).

Alison Allen is Research Manager at Heist (Higher Education Information Services Trust). Her research includes *The Careers Adviser – HE Interface* (Heist, 1994), *The International Student Experience* (Heist, 1994), *Higher Education in the College (FE) Sector* (Heist, 1995) and *Higher Education: The Ethnic Minority Experience* (with E Adia and D Roberts, Heist, 1996).

Paul Michael Allen has been teaching in further and higher education since 1988. He has worked as an Ethnic Minorities Liaison Officer and a Post-Graduate Research Assistant. Since completing his doctoral thesis in 1993, he has published articles concerning 'race' and higher education. He currently teaches sociology at Tile Hill College in Coventry.

Waqar Azmi is Director of Hereford and Worcester Racial Equality Council. In addition to the research published in this book, he has conducted in-depth research on ethnic relations in Southampton. Recent conference papers include 'Racist Bullying' (with T Acland, University of Hertfordshire, 1996) and 'Race and Higher Education' (Southampton, 1997).

Paul Dewart is a Consultant in Obstetrics and Gynaecology, St Johns Hospital, West Lothian NHS Trust, and was formerly a researcher at the University of Manchester.

Aneez Esmail is a Senior Lecturer, Department of General Practice, University of Manchester and currently a Visiting Professor of Social Medicine and The Commonwealth Fund Harkness Fellow, Harvard University Medical School. He has published a number of studies on racial discrimination and medical schools in the *British Medical Journal* and elsewhere.

David Gillborn is Reader in Sociology of Education at the University of London, Institute of Education, where he is Associate Director of the Health and Education Research Unit (HERU). He has researched and written extensively in the field of 'race' and ethnic relations in education. His most recent publications include *Racism and Antiracism in Real Schools* (Open University Press, 1995) and the influential report *Recent Research on the Achievements of Ethnic Minority Pupils* (with C Gripps, OFSTED, 1996). He is editor of the international journal *Race Ethnicity and Education*.

Alicear Jiwani is Head of the independent Community and Urban Research Consultancy (CURC) Unit in the Department of Education and Community Studies at the University of East London. She has over 20 years experience in research, monitoring and evaluation across a number of disciplines, spanning private industry and academia. She has carried out research for UEL on equal opportunities, ethnicity, culture, race and nationality, and acted as Research Projects Director for the Department, directing the monitoring and evaluation tracking project for Bethnal Green City Challenge.

Heidi Safia Mirza is Reader in Sociology and Director of post-graduate programme in social sciences at South Bank University, London. She has taught Afro-American studies at Brown University, USA, and researched on race and gender issues in the Caribbean and Britain. Her current research is on black women in higher education and the educational strategies of the black community in Britain and Africa. Her publications include *Young, Female and Black* (Routledge, 1992) and *Black British Feminism* (editor, Routledge, 1997). She has recently been appointed to the Government's School Standards Task Force.

Tariq Modood is Professor of Sociology, Politics and Public Policy at the University of Bristol. Prior to this he was a Programme Director at PSI. His recent publications include *Ethnic Minorities in Britain: Diversity and Disadvantage* (co-author, PSI, 1997), *Church, State and Religious Minorities* (editor, PSI, 1997), *Debating Cultural Hybridity* (joint editor, Zed Books, 1997) and *The Politics of Multiculturalism in the New Europe* (joint editor, Zed Books, 1997). He is currently leading a research project on ethnic minority staff in higher education.

Terry Regan is currently employed as a researcher with a local education authority and as a part-time Senior Researcher for CURC. He was a Research Fellow and the Unit's senior researcher, and worked on the monitoring and evaluation tracking project for Bethnal Green City Challenge, and the UEL project on equal opportunities, among others.

Gurharpal Singh is Principal Lecturer in Politics at De Montfort University, Leicester. His publications include *Communism in Punjab* (1994), *Punjabi Identity* (1996), *Region and Partition* (1998) and *Ethnic Conflict in India* (1998, forthcoming). Besides research on Indian politics, he has undertaken research on race and equal opportunities in the UK with reference to housing.

Ruth van Dyke is Course Director of the social science degree programme at South Bank University. She has worked on Equal Opportunities Curriculum issues at the Polytechnic of North London and for the Open University. She researches in the area of equal opportunities monitoring of student achievement and progression. She helped found the CRE's Monitoring Ethnic Minority Students Working Party, was a member of the CRE, EOC and CUCO steering group for the Higher Education and Equality guidelines in 1997, and is now a member of the CUCO Race and Ethnicity Task Group.

Acknowledgements

We would like to thank the Paul Hamlyn Trust, the Barrow Cadbury Trust and the Southampton Institute for their financial support for various aspects of this project.

Thanks are also due to Siân Putnam at PSI and Victoria Starr at the Southampton Institute for administrative support and to Karin Erskine and Jo O'Driscoll at PSI for turning the typescript into this book.

Chapter 1

Introduction:
Race and Higher Education

Tariq Modood and Tony Acland

This book addresses an issue of growing concern for educational policy-makers and researchers in contemporary Britain – race and higher education. Based mainly upon a collection of papers originally presented at a national conference jointly organised by the Policy Studies Institute and Southampton Institute in May 1996, the book examines the experience of ethnic minorities in the post-compulsory state education system.

The original conference was planned because the organisers believed that recent research suggested that there had been considerable change in the achievements and experiences of ethnic minorities in higher education during the last 20 years. The drive towards educational attainment, as measured by staying-on rates and applications to higher education, was becoming very high in all minority groups. However, it was also clear that the experience of minority groups in schools and higher education was diverse, with minority ethnic groups represented among the highest achievers as well as the most disadvantaged. It was also evident that social class and gender differences continued to be important factors which interacted with ethnicity to shape educational opportunities and outcomes.

PURPOSE AND AIMS

In reporting upon the contributions to the conference, the overall purpose of this book was to produce a clearer picture of the complexity of existing trends as a step towards reconceptualising the phenomenon of race and educational attainment. By focusing upon a range of different key variables and their interactions, the contributors have attempted to produce a better understanding of the processes of racial disadvantage and differential educational experience.

An important aim of this book was to produce a clearer analysis of the nature of race and higher education so that effective educational policies and intervention strategies can be devised. Indeed, research evidence cited in this text was submitted as evidence to the National Committee of Inquiry into Higher Education (1997) chaired by Sir Ron Dearing in order to contribute to the overall picture of changing participation rates and the experience of different social groups in higher education.

By providing both up-to-date research findings and critical analysis it is anticipated that this book will be important reading for all who are concerned with widening access to higher education. It should be of particular interest to:

- policy-makers with responsibility for equal opportunities in higher education, and those responsible for implementing policies;
- those interested in exploring the implications of multiculturalism in higher education institutions;
- academics interested in the latest research and analysis on race, ethnicity and higher education;
- students on teacher education and social science programmes who are interested in recent trends in educational attainment and disadvantage;
- equality professionals and educationalists;
- campaigning organisations concerned with race and equal opportunity.

STRUCTURE OF THE BOOK

In assembling contributions to this book, the editors have been mindful of the importance of including a wide range of recent research and analysis on race and higher education. Care has been taken to avoid focusing exclusively on a particular research approach or theoretical perspective.

An adequate understanding of the experiences of minority groups in higher education can only be based upon the appraisal of a range of different kinds of evidence and analysis. For this reason, contributions to the book reflect very different research methods and theoretical standpoints. In particular, readers are provided with analyses of a range of both quantitative and qualitative data which explore the nature and diversity of ethnic minority educational experience. In this way, the book provides both detailed analyses of the most recently available statistical data of educational participation rates as well as in-depth examinations of the perceptions and reported experiences of ethnic minorities in educational institutions.

This book has been organised to guide the reader through the key issues and debates concerning race and higher education. The book begins with an analysis of the continued salience of racist experience in schools which can shape educational attitudes and behaviour in later years. This is followed by a discussion of the most recently available evidence on the educational profiles of ethnic groups. The way in which Caribbean females effectively use the educational system to transform their lives is then explored. The book then centres on a series of chapters which examine the changing perceptions and experiences of ethnic minorities in higher education. The editors have been careful to include chapters based on national surveys together with in-depth case studies of particular higher education institutions.

Throughout the book contributors adopt a policy-oriented approach when exploring the implications of their research findings and analysis. The book concludes with a final chapter which reviews key points from each contribution and suggests a way forward by outlining appropriate educational strategies to improve the experience of ethnic minorities in higher education.

Readers will note that there is some divergence among authors on the appropriate terminology employed to identify the non-white racialised British population groups that are the subject of this book. This particularly affects the question as to who is 'black'. For Heidi Mirza (Chapter 4), for example, it is people of African-Caribbean ancestry, while for Paul Allen (Chapter 7) it includes South Asians. The generic term most employed in the book is 'ethnic minorities', the term that has come to achieve the most consensus in the last decade, while the specific group labels tend to approximate to those that have emerged through the categories that people have been willing to assign themselves on official forms, especially the 1991 census. These labels are politically contested and, being largely the products of disparate identity movements, are undergoing continual change as new identity claims emerge or old ones lose their power to unite (Modood, 1992; Modood et al, 1994). This being the case, we have hesitated to impose a uniform vocabulary but have simply ensured clarity in each chapter.

SUMMARY OF THE BOOK

Part One examines how aspects of race and ethnicity may shape educational progress. In Chapter 2 David Gillborn argues that ethnic minorities continue to experience significant levels of racism in schools, particularly in terms of ethnic stereotyping by other pupils and teachers. Based both on his own research in a multi-ethnic school in the English Midlands and his review of recent research on ethnic minority pupils' experiences, Gillborn argues that teachers, in particular, contribute to racist stereotyping. This is particularly the case as regards Caribbean pupils, for even when some white teachers appear to believe in equal opportunities, black students are disproportionately subject to control and criticism. Gillborn believes that teachers behave this way because they perceive black pupils to be a threat. Such experiences contribute to the relatively poor scholastic performance of Caribbean males, and perhaps black students who progress to higher education do so scarred by their racist experiences at school. He also shows that the racism suffered by Asians has to be differently understood from that of black pupils, for as far as teachers may be concerned it has a more ambivalent character, whilst it takes a more physically aggressive form in some white pupils' behaviour.

In Chapter 3 Tariq Modood analyses the results of a major national survey and the latest statistical information on higher education applications and entry. He notes that the overall trend is clear, with almost all ethnic minority groups overrepresented in higher education applications and entry statistics. However, he demonstrates that there are important ethnic group differences and that these are connected to gender differences within groups, to the educational backgrounds of older members of these groups and the degree to which groups pursue an academic or vocational orientation in seeking qualifications. Nevertheless, he believes that a general and growing drive for qualifications can be seen among all minority groups compared to their white peers.

In Chapter 4 Heidi Mirza offers a distinctive analysis of black women in education. She notes that, surprising as it may be to some, black females have been relatively successful in the British educational system – in some respects more so than white and other minority women. She examines the meaning and significance of such success levels for black women in society. Arguing from a black feminist perspective, she focuses upon 'the paradox of inclusive acts by excluded groups'. In this way, she discusses whether the success of black women can be simply attributed to a strong desire to conform to conventional meritocratic ideologies, or whether such apparently conformist behaviour can be reconceptualised as essentially subversive and transformative in the nature in which black women create and recreate their own lives.

Part Two focuses specifically on the attraction and alienation ethnic minorities experience as regards higher education institutions, and how institutions can take on board the concerns of ethnic minority applicants and students. In Chapter 5 Alison Allen outlines part of a national study of ethnic minorities in 30 British higher education institutions in 1995. She focuses upon the study's findings concerning the influences upon ethnic minority individuals when considering entry to higher education. She examines the differences between ethnic minorities and white groups according to the extent to which they and their parents valued higher education as a vehicle for upward social mobility. In addition, she explores contrasts between white and ethnic minority students in patterns of subject choice and the extent to which they focused upon new or old universities in their applications, and what it was about these institutions that attracted them.

Chapter 6 is the first of three chapters which complement the national survey by providing in-depth case studies of the experiences of ethnic minority students in higher education, each based on a single institution. Tony Acland and Waqar Azmi's analysis is based upon focus group discussions with South Asian, African and Caribbean undergraduates over a three-year period in the mid-1990s in a non-university institution. They explore the extent to which higher educational organisations provide adequate services and facilities for ethnic minority students. They also examine the quality of the learning environment for ethnic minorities, including evaluating the appropriateness of the curriculum and the persistence of racist experiences which can affect an ethnic minority person's life and achievements in higher education. They conclude with a discussion of the policy changes and strategies needed to improve the experience of ethnic minorities in higher education.

In Chapter 7 Paul Allen outlines the conclusions of his in-depth study of black students in a new university. He examines the perceptions and experiences of black undergraduates, particularly focusing upon issues of the curriculum, staffing, black informal networks, employment destinations and accessibility. Allen develops the concept of 'black scepticality' to explore the way in which black students generate their own critical attitude towards higher education and 'black space' because of their daily experiences of racism and dissatisfaction with a eurocentric curriculum.

In Chapter 8 Alicear Jiwani and Terry Regan conclude the in-depth case studies of higher educational institutions by outlining their research in a new university with a very high proportion of ethnic minority students. They employed both quantitative and qualitative research techniques to gather information from both staff and students. In this chapter they provide the aspect of their findings in relation to staff and students' views on whether the curriculum of different departments should reflect cultural, religious, racial and nationality issues. These questions are pursued to a level of detail and with sample sizes that make the findings particularly interesting, especially as the issue of the curriculum is one of the least discussed of topics to do with equal opportunities and yet may become more contested as multiculturalism becomes more debated. Or at least that has been the US experience where arguments about 'the canon' have become among the most prominent of the issues to do with race and multiculturalism in the country, especially among and between academics and students.

Finally, Part Three explores some of the ethnic hierarchies as a feature of higher educational institutions. Chapter 9 is the first of two studies which examine the experiences of ethnic minority under-graduates in examinations and other assessments, as well as their achievement rates compared to white students. Ruth van Dyke considers the way in which assessment processes may have differential consequences for the achievement rates of ethnic minorities and white groups of undergraduates. In her study of two new universities in London, she advocates the importance of carefully monitoring student retention, progression and achievement rates in higher education. Her research develops a new methodology to achieve this purpose. Van Dyke uses this methodology to demonstrate that important contrasts exist in achievement patterns between Asian and Caribbean undergraduates, as well as contrasts with patterns for white groups. She suggests that her monitoring methodology may help universities to identify the causes of ethnic differences in achievement rates, thereby aiding the development of effective strategies to redress inequalities.

In Chapter 10 Aneez Esmail and Paul Dewart report on a unique study which analysed the experience of ethnic minority students in their final clinical examination in a prestigious British medical school. Their study identifies some disturbing contrasts between the results of traditional written examinations and assessments which involve face-to-face interaction between ethnic minority students and their white academic assessors. Issues of ethnic stereotyping and discrimination are raised by this study, which concludes with an outline of the strategies adopted by the medical school to redress ethnic biases in the assessment process.

In Chapter 11 Gurharpal Singh discusses staffing and race equality policies in higher education institutions. At a time when higher education institutions admit students in large numbers from all ethnic minorities, Singh explores whether universities have been equally successful in promoting effective equal opportunity policies among academic and support staff. He cites several important industrial tribunal decisions of racial discrimination by a university and suggests that universities have so far taken too complacent a view about racial discrimination in staff recruitment and career development.

In the final chapter, Tariq Modood and Tony Acland explore the implications of the quantitative and qualitative analyses of the contributors to this book. They draw upon the main findings and conclusions of earlier chapters in order to provide an overview of the position and the experiences of ethnic minorities in higher education. They do not attempt to reduce the diverse contributions to a single set of conclusions, for as has been said, the contributors have different perspectives and emphases. Rather they show that the pattern that is emerging from this new field of research challenges the association of race and educational underachievement. The book shows that when it comes to the study of educational attainments and experiences there is no white–non-white divide. The categories that for the last two decades have constituted the bases of comparisons between groups, that have been taken to define educational research into race and ethnicity, may distort more than they reveal. Hence the research on race and higher education may have something to teach as well as to learn from the older, more established field of race and schools. The final section of this chapter focuses upon the key policy issues and dilemmas which confront policy-makers and outlines a strategy for improving the experience of ethnic minorities in higher education.

Part One

The Educational Progress
of Racialised Minorities

Chapter 2

Race and Ethnicity in Compulsory Schooling[1]

David Gillborn

In their attempts to enter higher education, many young people of ethnic minority background find themselves struggling to make best use of qualifications that do an injustice to their level of motivation and understanding but which were deemed more 'appropriate' (ie of lower status) by teachers and careers advisers during the years of compulsory schooling. Nevertheless, among the principal ethnic groups in Great Britain, white young people are the least likely to remain in full-time education beyond the age of 16: after controlling for levels of qualification, ethnic origin has been found to be the 'single most important variable in determining the chances of staying on' (Drew, Gray and Sime, 1992: 12). Such data are clear testament to minority students' determination to succeed in an education system which (despite its historical failure to provide equal opportunities) continues to be seen by many as the most effective way of combating racism in the employment market (by offering credentials that may make a difference).

Higher education has remained largely absent from the growing literature on the operation of race and ethnicity in the British educational system. Although researchers are now gathering more sensitive and detailed information about access to courses of different status and in different parts of the system (see, for example, Modood and Shiner, 1994), the operation of racism – as a daily, oppressive force – has received relatively little direct attention: John Bird's recently published book, *Black Students and Higher Education* (Bird, 1996), stands as an exceptional contribution.

[1]   A longer version of this paper was originally prepared for a meeting of the American Anthropological Association. Reprinted here with permission from *Anthropology & Education Quarterly*, Vol 28, No 3. With special thanks to Kathryn M Anderson-Levitt.

There are good reasons, therefore, for considering the growing literature on race and ethnicity in the years of compulsory schooling. This research offers a detailed and powerful account of the ways that racism operates on a commonsense level to deny equal opportunities to many young people of ethnic minority background. The work demonstrates that race and racism mean different things in different contexts and for different groups: all ethnic minority groups may experience racism, but they do not necessarily all experience racism of the same kind nor magnitude. This chapter reviews some of the most important findings to emerge from the qualitative literature on the school experiences of black and ethnic minority students: the particular focus is on the schooling of young people from African-Caribbean and South Asian ethnic backgrounds.[2] The research suggests that racism is common place and routine: in studies of primary and secondary schools alike, teachers' notions of race and ethnicity have important consequences for the lives of all students. The work highlights many issues that have consequences for, and parallels within, the world of higher education.

THE SCHOOL EXPERIENCES OF
AFRICAN CARIBBEAN STUDENTS

Although qualitative research has been established for some time, it is only fairly recently that ethnic diversity has become a major focus. Since the mid-1980s an increasing literature has explored ethnicity and educational experience in institutions covering the entire age range of compulsory schooling. These studies add a vital dimension to work on achievement and educational opportunity; previously researchers usually sought explanations that focused on minority children and/or their families and communities (see Troyna and Carrington, 1990). By examining the significance of race and ethnicity in the daily lives of schools, qualitative researchers have begun to build a more detailed and contextual understanding of how racism can operate within school settings.

---

2   There are, of course, no universally accepted means of identifying and naming the various social groups commonly constructed as 'racial' and/or ethnic minorities. Notwithstanding the use of different terms in previous work, wherever possible I try to adopt categories that the people so labelled recognise and accept: for this reason I use the term 'black' with reference to people of African-Caribbean ethnic background but *not* for those with family origins in South Asia.

The interaction between white teachers and African-Caribbean students was central to some of the first qualitative research on ethnicity in British schools and remains a major concern. Additionally, researchers have charted some of the ways black young people respond to their school experiences. Both questions have direct bearing on school performance.

Black students are frequently portrayed as conflicting with the behavioural requirements of mainstream schools. Historically they are more likely to be moved into separate schools and units for those deemed to have special emotional, learning and behavioural problems (Cooper et al, 1991; Tomlinson, 1981). Also they are more often subject to 'permanent exclusion' (expulsion) from school. This is the single most serious sanction available to headteachers; less than one in three students return to full-time mainstream education following a permanent exclusion (DfE, 1992). Recent data suggest that black students are between four and six times more likely to be excluded than their white peers (Gillborn and Gipps, 1996; DfEE, 1997). Although older boys (aged 14 to 15) are most likely to be excluded, in comparison with peers of the same age and/or gender, African-Caribbean girls and young women are also excluded in dispro-portionate numbers (Gillborn, 1996). Ethnographies of multi-ethnic schools suggest that statistics like these may be the tip of an iceberg; even where they share the same classroom as other students, teachers' beliefs and actions can be such that African-Caribbean young people do not enjoy equal opportunities to succeed.

Qualitative research frequently points to a relatively high level of tension, even conflict, between white teachers and African-Caribbean students. This finding emerged in one of the first detailed studies of a multi-ethnic secondary school (Driver, 1979) and was repeated a decade later in research on two comprehensive schools (Wright, 1986). Both researchers found that African-Caribbean students were disciplined by teachers more often than their peers of other ethnic backgrounds. Cecile Wright's work also illustrated the degree to which teacher/student relations could deteriorate where white teachers blamed black youth for a perceived decline in school standards of achievement and behaviour. Her accounts revealed a degree of insensitivity and antagonism that had not been documented previously. Maírtín Mac an Ghaill's (1988) study, of a boy's school and Further Education college, confirmed Wright's account of deeply felt conflict between white teachers and black students. However, Mac an Ghaill's more thorough attention to the range of teacher perspectives was especially notable. He demonstrated that even well-intentioned 'liberal' teachers often displayed negative and patronising views of black students as disadvantaged by broken homes and pathological family structures.

Mac an Ghaill also noted that, despite their shared position as ethnic minorities, African-Caribbean and Asian students were subject to different stereotypes. 'Asian male students [tend] to be seen by the teachers as technically of "high ability" and socially conformist' while African-Caribbeans are 'seen as having "low ability" and potential discipline problems' (Mac an Ghaill, 1988: 64). This leads to a situation where the same action, say borrowing equipment from a friend, may be legitimate for Asian students but labelled 'disruptive' for African-Caribbeans (Mac an Ghaill, 1988: 66).

In my study of City Road Comprehensive,[3] a multi-ethnic school in the English Midlands, I observed similar behaviour by teachers. Black students were disproportionately controlled and criticised, not because they broke clear school rules any more frequently, but because teachers perceived them as a threat (Gillborn, 1990). And yet City Road teachers, unlike those studied by Wright and Mac an Ghaill, did not speak about the school in terms that suggested black students were responsible for any fall in standards. Indeed, during two years fieldwork I discovered that the majority of teachers were highly committed to the goal of equality of opportunity. Some younger teachers had deliberately chosen the school because they wanted to teach in the inner-city. Nevertheless, classroom observations, interviews with students (of all ethnic backgrounds) and an analysis of school punishment records confirmed that, as a group, black students (of both sexes) were disproportionately criticised by white teachers. Despite the teachers' genuine concern to work with all students, therefore, for African-Caribbean young people teacher/student interaction was fraught with conflict and suspicion.

Ethnographic data on teachers' beliefs about working in an inner-city school, plus an analysis of interactions where black students were punished for displays of their ethnicity – their sense of difference and ethnic identity – revealed that teachers frequently operated according to a myth concerning a black challenge to authority. Teachers believed that African-Caribbean students, as a group, presented a greater threat to classroom order and their personal safety. They expected trouble from black students, sometimes perceived a threat where none was intended, and reacted quickly (as they saw it) to prevent further challenges. Consequently,

---

3   City Road Comprehensive is a wholly fictitious pseudonym.

well-intentioned and committed teachers came to recreate familiar patterns of control and conflict with African-Caribbean students. Although the myth of a black challenge was rarely stated explicitly, its consequences were felt lesson-by-lesson, day-by-day. A frequent recipient of teachers' reprimands, for example, was Paul Dixon; a black student who was widely seen as wasting his high ability through adopting 'the wrong attitude'. On one occasion Paul and his close friend Arif Aslam (a young man of Pakistani background) arrived together seven minutes late for a lesson. They went directly to the teacher and apologised for the delay, explaining that they had been talking with a senior member of staff. Almost half an hour into the lesson, and like the rest of the class, Paul and Arif were holding a low-level conversation as they worked. The teacher looked up from the student he was with and shouted across the room:

> Paul. Look, you come in late, now you have the audacity to waste not only your time but his [Arif's] as well.

The fact that the students had arrived together and were sharing a conversation was lost: the teacher's statement explicitly constructed the black student as a time-waster and bad influence, while his Asian friend was placed in the role of blameless victim.

In analysing the teachers' beliefs about black students in City Road I described their perspective as a myth because it relied on (and reconstructed) a distorted view of the world – a fiction. Yet, like all persistent myths, it drew strength from both the past and the present. The view of black people as physically powerful and prone to violence was, of course, a key feature of the thinking that supported and excused the slave trade: modern versions of this stereotype are endlessly recreated (with varying subtlety) in the popular media and beyond (cf Mirza, 1998; Solomos and Back, 1996; Van Dijk, 1991).

Within the school, the myth of a black challenge was handed down (sometimes overtly, often tacitly) from one generation to another as part of the craft knowledge of white teachers, and recreated through the (mis)interpretation of contemporary events. When criticised, for example, some students with family origins in the Caribbean turn their eyes away from teachers' gaze; it has been argued that this is a cultural trait signifying respect (Driver 1979). Yet white teachers frequently see the action as a rejection of their authority, leading to further conflict. It should also be noted, however, that black students have also found themselves criticised for *not* averting their gaze: a sign of insolence in some teachers' eyes. In any event, black young people frequently find themselves in receipt of teachers' criticism for actions whose meaning to the student may be varied and complex, but for the teacher are invested with simple rejection/threat. One of Paul's teachers, for example, told me the following:

> I think he's got it in for white[...] When you're talking to him he's going...
>
> [the teacher looks away, feigning apparent lack of interest]
>
> You know, you can see him thinking, 'What right have you got – a white – to tell *me* off'.

It is especially significant that this teacher sees the rejection of his authority as a racial issue. It is not about age, or experience, or knowledge – in the teacher's mind the key issue is race: he feels the threat as a white. Within City Road Comprehensive this view of black students, as a threat to the teachers' authority, was generalised onto the entire group:

> [Several teachers are discussing a local news item about the dis-proportionate expulsion of African Caribbean students. Kathy, a teacher who is generally well liked by the students, notes:]
>
> I've never been assaulted by a white kid.
>
> I've been thrown against a wall by a pupil and it was a black kid.
>
> I've been called a 'fucking slag' but I've only ever been *hit* by a black kid.

This statement, by a usually compassionate and dedicated teacher, shows how any single incident could be taken and used to damn all black students, in this case suggesting that while many urban students might resort to verbal abuse, blacks are somehow more capable of physical assault.

Successive ethnographies of urban schooling in the UK have concluded that African-Caribbean students experience school in ways that are different from – more conflict-ridden than – students of other ethnic groups. In addition to studies of secondary schools (Foster, 1990; Gillborn, 1990; Mac an Ghaill, 1988; Mirza, 1992; Sewell, 1997; Wright, 1986) a similar pattern has been documented in the early years and in primary classes (Connolly, 1995; Epstein, 1993; Troyna and Hatcher, 1992; Wright, 1992). In all of this, only one researcher has concluded that the teachers' actions were simply legitimate responses to clear differences in the behaviour of black students (Foster, 1990).[4]

An important trend in research on the school experiences of black students, therefore, has been to shift the focus away from teachers' conscious intentions and onto the consequences of their actions. In this way, qualitative research has begun to explore how racism can operate in subtle and more widespread forms than the crude, often violent attitudes that are usually associated with notions such as prejudice and discrimination. This situation affects black students of either sex. However, this is not to say that gender is unimportant. Young African-Caribbean women experience school differently, in some ways, to their male counterparts. Several qualitative studies (Fuller, 1980; Mac an Ghaill, 1988, 1989; Mirza, 1992) have explored the consequences of gender/race stereotypes in detail. Young black women are often subject to stereotypes of loud boisterousness, for example, that can lead to opportunities being closed down:

> Take Maxine last year, I had her name pencilled in for the A band [the highest ability teaching group]. What happened? It turned out that there were two girls to choose from; one was Maxine, a noisy West Indian girl, and the other, a quiet white girl. Guess who got the vote? Mr S [a teacher] said Maxine didn't deserve to get the A band. I saw her work recently and she's gone backwards. (A teacher, quoted in Middleton 1983: 88)

The greatest inequalities, however, may have their roots in the racialised and sexualised discourses that surround white teachers' views of young black men. Black boys tend to achieve less highly, and are more likely to be expelled, than their female counterparts (Gillborn and Gipps, 1996). Both Mac an Ghaill (1988, 1989) and Sewell (1997) argue that different peer and teacher pressures may amplify male resistance in ways that lead to more serious disciplinary responses (such as expulsion). In this way, recent ethnographies of black male peer groups highlight the dilemmas faced by students where the very masculinity that seems to offer them respect among peers (including whites) feeds directly into actions that will fail them in school (Mac an Ghaill, 1994; Sewell, 1995; 1997). These studies are important because they begin to unpack the complex interplay of forces at the school level: black youth are not simply powerless victims, they retain a strong sense of their own identity and agency, and yet they can come to play out

---

4   For contrasting discussions of the issues raised by Foster's work see Gillborn (1995, Chapter 3) and Hammersley (1995, Chapter 4).

exactly the roles written for them in white fantasies of black male violence/sexuality: 'They are the images that the dominant culture finds easiest to accept, process and take pleasure in' (Gilroy, 1993: 35).

Although qualitative studies of male student subculture have addressed the role of masculinity in school failure, they are mostly silent on the topic of success. Existing research on successful black students tends to focus on black girls and young women (cf Fuller, 1980; Mac an Ghaill, 1988; Mirza, 1992, 1997): this work has established that high academic performance does not necessarily entail rejection of ethnicity nor simple conformity. In many cases the students adopted an instrumental view of education (as the means to an end) and were highly critical of their schools and teachers. A simple dichotomy between resistance and conformity is, therefore, too crude (Aggleton and Whitty, 1985). Mac an Ghaill (1988) uses the notion of 'resistance *within* accommodation' to describe the strategies of the successful black and Asian young women in his study. There are some parallels between Mac an Ghaill's study of 'the black sisters' and my own account of the school career of Paul Dixon (the highest achieving black male in City Road). In both cases the students adopted strategies that involved great personal sacrifice and a weakening of previously valued friendships. Yet both cases also concern students who retained a sense of themselves as young black people whilst managing relationships with teachers so as to minimise possible conflict. In Paul's case, however, resistance was achieved through the act of educational success itself – unlike Mac an Ghaill's black sisters, even limited signs of resistance (through lateness or minor disobedience) were absent.

A range of responses are also evident in Sewell's (1997) research on Township School, a boys' comprehensive, where he examines in detail the multiple forces working on, and through, black male subcultural responses to schooling. Sewell's research is significant in many ways, not least for the attention he gives to 'conformist' students among his interviewees. Sewell's data demonstrate the complex and often painful demands made upon young black men trying to succeed in a system that sees them as alien and dangerous. He documents their struggles with black peers, as well as white teachers, as the 'conformists' make the 'cultural sacrifice' necessary for success. This is an important addition to the field and signals the need more obviously to focus on the nature of success and conformity in masculine peer groups – an area where the construction of acceptable sexualities can often lead to the remaking of black exclusion and educational failure. There are too few studies, but it seems that academically ambitious black males have even less room for manoeuvre with black peers and white teachers than their female counterparts. Clearly this is an area where additional qualitative research is vitally important.

THE SCHOOL EXPERIENCES OF SOUTH ASIAN STUDENTS

South Asian students make up a heterogeneous grouping within British schools. Asian communities are internally differentiated along many lines: most important are national, religious, linguistic, caste and economic factors. Certain locally-based statistics suggest significant variation in the average performance of different Asian groups; notably, children of Indian parentage seem consistently to achieve relatively higher results. In contrast, Bangladeshi students often perform less well than other Asian groups (Tomlinson, 1992; Gillborn and Gipps, 1996). Many factors have been suggested as potentially contributing to this pattern, including linguistic competence, cultural attitudes towards educational certification, and socioeconomic characteristics; it is known, for example, that the Indian population of Britain is relatively skewed towards a higher social class profile, while the Bangladeshi population suffers disproportionate levels of economic disadvantage (Modood et al, 1997). Unfortunately, many surveys still use aggregate approaches that lose sight of differences within the Asian population. Ethnographic research is less prone to this failing, although the small, specific nature of qualitative sampling restricts our ability to generalise. In relation to the school experiences and performance of South Asian students, to date qualitative research has been most valuable in highlighting previously hidden aspects of the students' interaction with white teachers and peers.

Qualitative research has revealed widespread patronising and racist stereotypes that can operate to close down educational opportunities for young Asian people. Teachers frequently assume Asian communities to be excessively authoritarian; emphasising narrow, restrictive expectations for their children, who are raised in families thought to be dominated (sometimes violently) by the rule of the father. Such views can lead teachers to lower their expectations of Asian students, especially young women, because they expect their lives to be restricted by overly protective families, the spectre of early marriage and the demands of home. Such perspectives can surface even in the most routine interactions:

> The teacher was distributing letters to the class to take home to parents
> to elicit their permission [for a forthcoming school trip]. The teacher
> commented to the Asian girls in the class. 'I suppose we'll have
> problems with you girls. Is it worth me giving you a letter, because your
> parents don't allow you to be away from home overnight?' (Wright,
> 1992: 18)

This is a complex area, where reliable data on parents' true feelings
are scarce. Interviews with 55 young Muslim women, predominantly
of Pakistani background, indicated that around a third of parents
were unequivocally opposed to their daughters pursuing higher
education (Brah and Shaw, 1992: 43). Research on Punjabi Sikhs in
the UK, however, shows that extended education for young women
is actively encouraged by parents, and is supported by community
norms that place a premium on women's education (Bhachu, 1985).
Teacher stereotypes, concerning a lack of support for the education
of young Asian women, are therefore exaggerations at best, and at
worst diametrically opposite to the true situation (depending on
specific cultural and local factors) (Gibson and Bhachu, 1988).

It has already been noted that whereas African-Caribbean
students are often perceived as loud, aggressive and academically
poor, young men of South Asian background tend to be seen
differently; as 'technically of "high ability" and socially conformist'
(Mac an Ghaill, 1988: 64). This is carried to further extremes in
teachers' views of Asian young women. Here a stereotype of
passivity, of the 'docile' Asian girl, 'has often meant that the girls are
systematically forgotten or ignored when it comes to demands on the
teachers' time' (Brah and Minhas, 1985: 19). In some classrooms
Asian young women are, in effect, invisible. In the eyes of their
white peers, however, Asian girls are all too visible. A significant
contribution of qualitative research in this field has been to expose
the almost routine nature of racial violence and harassment in
schools, including those with few minority students.

> One of the most common interactions we have in the playground, the
> most common, widely used abuse is 'You dirty Paki' or 'Fuck off, Paki'.
> (A local authority officer, quoted in Gillborn, 1992: 162).

Such findings contrast sharply with the outcomes of quantitative
approaches. Smith and Tomlinson (1989), for example, found 'little
indication of overt racism' in their survey of 18 comprehensive
schools; yet a simultaneous ethnographic study of one of the same
schools found that 'racist attacks (usually, but not always, verbal)
were a regular fact of life for most Asian pupils...' (Gillborn, 1990:

78). By including participant observation and interviews with a range of students (both victims and aggressors) qualitative researchers have highlighted the importance of ethnicity within student subcultures – racist harassment is recognised as more than simple name-calling. As a white primary student notes:

> If I call someone 'dickhead' it doesn't really hurt them, but if I call someone a 'black bastard', something like that, that would hurt them. (Troyna and Hatcher, 1992: 168)

Unfortunately, qualitative research suggests that even when teachers witness acts of racist harassment they do not always react appropriately. Often such events are not even treated as bullying (increasingly recognised as a major problem in schools), rather they are dismissed as acts of boisterousness or mock aggression. The teachers' response (or lack of it) sends clear signals to students about the significance of 'race' and ethnicity in their schools.

Racist harassment – *in the playground:*

> I attended a middle school where approximately 90 per cent of the pupils were white... The Asians were constantly in fear of being attacked by the several gangs of white boys. As we ran towards the staff room a teacher would come out and disperse the white gang, throw us back into the playground and then walk back in as if nothing had happened. The teachers had no idea of what we were experiencing. (quoted in Swann, 1985: 34)

Racist harassment – *in the classroom:*

> [there is a good deal of aggressive *verbal* interaction within this group of pupils but the only recipients of *physical* violence are Asian pupils]

> At the end of the lesson [Ian Taylor – white] was collecting the pupils' exercise books when he moved around behind Sadiq, put his left hand on the back of Sadiq's head and tried to force the Asian pupil's face onto his desk. Sadiq [known as one of the physically weakest pupils in the group] took no other action than to brace himself and resist the pressure: he did not actually try to stop Taylor. The teacher saw what was happening and immediately ended the incident with a sarcastic, 'Ian... Collect the papers, don't bang Sadiq on the desk – he's small enough as it is.' (Classroom observation notes, Gillborn, 1990: 76)

Once again, qualitative research has identified important inter-connections between race, ethnicity, gender and sexuality. The harassment of Asian girls and young women, for example, frequently embodies a range of complex, sometimes contradictory, racist and sexist stereotypes (as at once demure yet licentious, alluring yet ugly):

> If I'm with a white boy, say just on the way home from college, they shout in the street, 'What's it like to fuck a Paki?', or if I'm on my own with other girls it's, 'Here comes the Paki whore, come and fuck us Paki whore, we've heard you're really horny'. Or maybe they'll put it the other way round, saying that I am dirty, that no one could possibly want to go to bed with a Paki... I don't think any white person can possibly identify with what it's like. (quoted in Brah, 1992: 73)

The complex interplay of variables such as class, ethnicity, gender and region is illuminated through a range of qualitative research. Mac an Ghaill (1988, 1989), for example, shows not only that Asian (Pakistani and Indian) males are as capable of resistance as their African-Caribbean peers, but also that social class differences influence the form of adaptation. Bhachu (1985) documents the dynamic character of Sikh life in Britain, where dominant values and customs reflect both community origins in the Punjab and experience of urban life and work in the UK.

Qualitative research also points to ways in which Asian students' school experiences may vary according to the ethnic composition of their schools. Although many white teachers hold negative views of Asian communities (as rigidly ordered, static and patriarchal) the particular manifestations of these views are not always the same (see Figure 2.1). Specifically, where African-Caribbean students make up a significant proportion of the school population, teachers' stereotypes of Asians can prove relatively positive: in contrast to their black peers, Asians are assumed to benefit from family support and a settled home life that complement the aims of the school. However, where Asians are the dominant ethnic group there is evidence to suggest that, in the absence of black students, the same basic stereotypes are differently articulated – in negative ways. In these cases Asians' actions may be seen as 'sly' rather than studious and the home community viewed as oppressive rather than supportive (Gillborn and Gipps, 1996; Mac an Ghaill, 1989; Shepherd, 1987).

CONCLUSIONS

Research highlights the variability of educational performance both *between* and *within* minority groups: Asian students, for example, perform more highly on average than their African-Caribbean peers; but each group is internally differentiated, particularly along lines of social class and gender, in ways that are also associated with variations in attainment (Gillborn and Gipps, 1996). One constant,

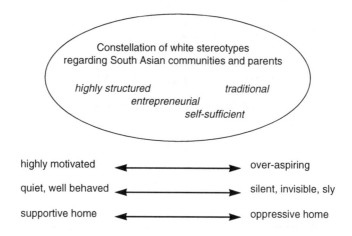

Figure 2.1   *The constitution of particular stereotypes
in different school contexts*

however, is the salience of ethnicity as a crucial factor in students'
school lives. Qualitative research, in particular, points to the importance of racism as a complex, changing and widespread factor that can
work against ethnic minority students in many different ways. Such
work identifies interconnections between forms of oppression that
can cut across each other in unpredictable ways; a combination of
race/sex stereotypes, for example, may make educational success
especially difficult for young African-Caribbean men. Similarly,
although South Asian students suffer disproportionate levels of
verbal and physical harassment, and can be subject to a range of
stereotypes, under certain conditions those same stereotypes can
operate to support positive teacher/student interactions where white
teachers view Asians as more settled and studious than their black
classmates. In this way, empirical work at the school level provides a
further impetus to recent attempts to theorise 'race' and ethnicity as
part of a more fluid and complex arena of socially constructed
identities and oppressions (Hall, 1992; McCarthy, 1990; McCarthy
and Apple, 1988; Omi and Winant, 1994; Rattansi, 1992). It is certain
that these same processes are at work throughout the educational
system, including the earliest stages and the most advanced levels of
post-compulsory study. In particular, there is an urgent need for
greater attention to be focused on the implications of ethnic diversity
for policy and practice throughout higher education.

Chapter 3

Ethnic Minorities' Drive
for Qualifications

One of the main stimuli to research on the educational attainments of non-white ethnic minority groups was the concern in the 1970s that children from these groups were 'underachieving' in schools. This concern culminated in the research undertaken for the Committee of Inquiry chaired initially by Anthony Rampton and later by Lord Swann. The broad finding was that children of West Indian origin were indeed less likely to achieve examination passes than their white peers but there was little difference between white and Asian children (Swann, 1985). Contemporaneous studies found that South Asians were likely to be over-represented, rather than under-represented in British universities (Vellins, 1982; Ballard and Vellins, 1985). Yet researchers and others concerned with racial equality found it difficult to accept these conclusions in relation to Asians.

There were at least two reasons for this. Firstly, it did not at all tally with the experience of some Asian communities and their educators. Secondly, anti-racists were inclined to assume that racial disadvantage and racism were primarily responsible for the under-achievement in qualification levels, and that this racism was of a common form. While the first response pointed towards diversity, distinguishing between different South Asian groups and their circumstances, the second assumption led many to talk about 'the black experience' as if what was true for Caribbeans must be true for all non-white groups and so Caribbean underrepresentation in higher education was generalised to all ethnic minority groups in spite of contrary evidence (CRE, 1991; Skellington and Morris, 1992; THES editorial, 5 July 1991; Bird et al, 1992a).

The inclination towards diversity was indeed the correct one. Not because racism is not real and makes no difference to educational opportunities and performance, but because even racism takes multiple forms (Modood, 1997). This is particularly evident from ethnographic research in schools and among young people. As David Gillborn's review of the relevant research in the previous chapter showed, the racism that Caribbean men and women experience is radically different from the racism that Asians experience, both in terms of the character of the racism and in terms of who is doing what to whom. The differences in the educational profiles of the different minority groups have become incontrovertible and have become a central characteristic of the field of study as data have accumulated through local education authority statistics (Gillborn and Gipps, 1996), the Labour Force Survey (Jones, 1993), the 1991 Census (Owen, 1993; Owen, Mortimore and Phoenix, 1997), and above all through the data collection instituted by the universities (Taylor, 1992a; Modood, 1993). These large data-sets have made it very clear that it is quite mistaken to equate non-white groups with low qualifications and scholastic alienation; indeed, the new research agenda has to include the explanation for the academic success of certain minorities and the over-representation in higher education of nearly all the minorities.

THE FOURTH SURVEY

In this chapter I would like to delineate and briefly explore this diversity as it manifests itself in the latest nationally representative sample of ethnic minorities, the Fourth National Survey of Ethnic Minorities, of which I was the principal researcher. Fieldwork was undertaken in 1994 and covered many topics besides educational qualifications, including employment, earnings and income, families, housing, health, racial harassment and cultural identity.

The survey was based on interviews, of roughly about an hour in length, conducted by ethnically matched interviewers, and offered in five South Asian languages and Chinese as well as English. Over 5,000 people were interviewed from the following six groups: African-Caribbeans, Indians, African-Asians, Pakistanis, Bangladeshis and Chinese. Additionally, nearly 3,000 white people were interviewed, in order to compare the circumstances of the minorities with those of the ethnic majority. Further details on all aspects of the survey are available in Modood et al, 1997.

QUALIFICATIONS: STARTING-POINTS AND PROGRESS

Table 3.1 compares the qualification levels of white and ethnic minority people of working age, with separate comparisons between men and women. Two measures are used. The first compares the number in each group without a qualification, the second compares those with degrees. In both cases the whites are taken as the baseline and normed as 1.0 and each minority group is shown in relation to whites. Nearly a third of white men have no qualifications and the table shows that non-white men fall into two groups: the position of Indians, African-Asians and Chinese is about the same as whites, but the position of Caribbean, Pakistani and, especially, Bangladeshi men is much worse. Just over a third of white women have no qualifications, about the same as Indians, while Caribbean, African-Asian and, especially, Chinese women are more likely to have a qualification. On the other hand, Pakistani and Bangladeshi women are as disproportionately without qualifications as men from those groups.

Table 3.1   Two qualification levels of people of working age

	White*	Caribbean	Indian	African-Asian	Pakistani	Bangladeshi	Chinese	All ethnic minorities
None or below O-level								
Men	1.0	1.4	1.1	1.0	1.5	1.8	0.9	1.2
Women	1.0	0.9	1.0	0.8	1.6	1.8	0.6	0.7
Degree (1991 Census)								
Men	1.0	0.4	--- 1.5 ---		0.8	0.7	2.2	1.1
Women	1.0	0.6	--- 1.4 ---		0.6	0.4	5.0	1.2

Base: Men 16–64 years; Women 16–59 years

*   Whites are normed as 1.0 and each minority group is shown in relation to whites.

When we compare these populations for university degrees the picture changes somewhat. Among men, the Caribbeans are least likely to have a degree, but Pakistanis and Bangladeshis are also underrepresented compared to white men. Yet, Indians/African-Asians and especially the Chinese are much more likely than white men to have degrees. The position among women is very similar except that the relative position of Caribbean women is a bit better and the position of the Chinese is outstanding.

These two measures show that the ethnic minorities are far from having a single qualifications profile. The discrepancy, incidentally, between the two measures is partly explained by gender differences between groups and by a greater internal polarisation within South Asian groups, who had a tendency to cluster at both ends of the qualifications hierarchy (Modood et al, 1997). A further factor accounting for this discrepancy was that in the pursuit of qualifications some groups were more vocationally than academically qualified, and so the qualified among them were less likely to have degrees. This was particularly the case with the Caribbeans and whites, who were much more likely to have a higher vocational qualification than the South Asian groups, who had a stronger academic orientation (Modood et al, 1997: 65–66).

What is the point of this analysis? This analysis takes as its base the adult population rather than school students or the university population in order to show that the differences between groups is not a product of some recent expansion in university admissions or, even, schools, for these differences predate educational developments in the UK. The qualification profiles of these populations, at the time of migration and now, are quite diverse. Some minority groups are proportionally less qualified than their white peers, and some much more so. This pattern is complicated by an ethnically-mediated gender, and by the differential academic-vocational orientations as well as other factors. The important point is that when it comes to the study of qualifications and educational experiences there is no white–non-white divide. Nor is there a white–Caribbean–Asian tripartite divide. The categories that for the last two decades have constituted the bases of comparisons between groups, that have been taken to define educational research into race and ethnicity, distort more than they reveal.

Let us pursue this further by tracking the progress in qualification levels across the generations. So far we have looked at a single snapshot of the working-age population. If however we look at the same comparisons over time we will begin to see to what extent the profiles today are due to differential starting points and to differential educational experiences. Figure 3.1 shows the proportion among the minority groups without qualifications divided into three 'generations':

1.   the migrants, those who came to Britain over the age of 16;
2.   the second generation, those who came to Britain under the age of 16 and so had some schooling in Britain, or were born in Britain, and are now between 25 and 44 years old;

3. the new generation, those who are between 16 and 24 years old,
    most of whom were born in Britain and had most if not all of their
    education in Britain.[1]

Strictly speaking, these are not generations as there could be an age
overlap between (1) and (2), and the years are not evenly spread
across the three categories.

Beginning with the migrant generation, we see in Figure 3.1 that
the six minority groups covered by the Fourth Survey fall into two
groupings. The Caribbeans, Pakistanis and the Bangladeshis had high
proportions without GCSE or equivalent qualifications, between 60
and 75 per cent. On the other hand, only about 45–50 per cent of
Indian, African-Asians and Chinese migrants were without this level
of qualifications. All six groups, however, have made educational
progress, though among Bangladeshis it is only among the young
that the proportion without qualifications has declined. I appreciate
that the following may run somewhat counter to expectations, but in
this Fourth Survey sample it was the Caribbeans (taking men and
women together) that initially made the most progress. This meant
that the second generation Caribbeans were no longer in the same
band as Pakistanis and Bangladeshis but had caught up with the
other minorities and, in fact, their white peers. As already stated, I
recognise that this finding about Caribbeans may be counter-intuitive
at first but may seem more reasonable if some points are borne in
mind. Caribbean migrants, even those without qualifications, unlike
the Asians, had English as their first tongue; moreover, the qualified
may not have been very highly qualified but they had British qualifications, while most of the other groups had qualifications from their
home countries. Hence the Caribbeans were just the migrant group
that one would expect to make most initial progress. Especially if we
recall that what we are discussing here is not the acquisition of a
high level qualification but the possession of any qualification at all. It
should, however, be added that we are here considering an average
covering both sexes. That Caribbean women were more likely than
other women to have a qualification certainly contributed to the good
overall average achieved by the second generation Caribbeans. By
the time of today's 16–2-year-olds, the gender gap has widened to

---

1   Of course many 16–24-year-olds will not have acquired their highest
qualification at this age and so while their qualifications levels can be
compared to their peers, they cannot be compared with their elders. The
method used here probably disproportionately understates the qualification
progress of the South Asians (see Modood et al, 1997: 72–73).

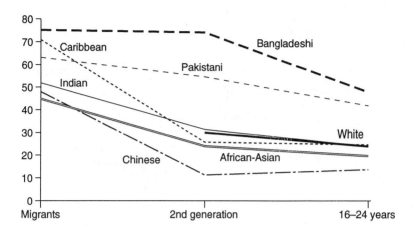

Figure 3.1 *Per cent within ethnic groups with no GCSE or equivalent qualifications, by generation*

the point that while exactly the same proportion of whites and Caribbeans have no qualifications (a quarter), with white women a little more likely than men not to, among Caribbeans nearly a third of men have no qualification compared to a sixth of the women.

It is, however, the Pakistanis and the Bangladeshis who have made the least progress in reducing the proportion within the group with no qualifications. While among all other groups about a fifth to a quarter had no GCSEs (it may have been much lower among the Chinese – cell sizes are too small for confidence), the proportions among these two groups was about double this. What Figure 3.1 shows then is, in terms of having no qualifications, most of the ethnic minority groups was similarly or better placed than their white peers, and that this is not something that has just been achieved recently but has been true for some time and partly reflects migrants' starting points. The groups who are worse placed than whites are the Bangladeshis, Pakistanis and Caribbean males.

Figure 3.1, however, is only part of the jigsaw. What is perhaps more important to look at is not those who have a qualification but those who have higher qualifications. Figure 3.2 presents the generational progress in relation to those who have an A-level or higher qualification. Once again three migrant groups stand out as well qualified, namely, the Chinese, African-Asians and Indians. And three groups were much less well qualified, the Bangladeshis especially, but also the Pakistanis and the Caribbeans. Again, all groups except

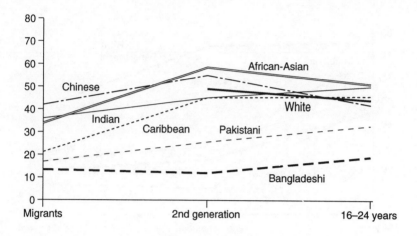

Figure 3.2　　*Per cent within ethnic groups with A-level or higher qualifications, by generation*

the Bangladeshis made progress in the second generation, though the progress of the Pakistanis was quite minor. Once again the Caribbeans made the most dramatic progress though the African Asians were the best qualified at this level in the country, considerably ahead of whites. What Figure 3.2 does not show is that while all other groups, even the Bangladeshis, were well represented at degree level, very few Caribbeans with higher level qualifications had degrees (just 2 per cent of the migrants and 7 per cent of the second generation). Many of their higher qualifications were vocational qualifications like HNCs or in nursing. In contrast, nearly 10 per cent of Pakistani and Bangladeshi migrants and a quarter of Indian, African-Asian and Chinese migrants had degrees. This meant that some groups like the Pakistanis and Bangladeshis were very internally polarised, with disproportionate numbers of highly qualified and unqualified. But it meant that all these groups had significant proportions of university educated persons. It is therefore not surprising that these groups have gone on to be well represented in higher education in their second and third generations. That they have not all made equal progress in this regard can partly be correlated to the extent that they had British or overseas qualifications. Thus the relatively limited progress of second generation Indians may be a reflection of the fact that the migrants disproportionately had Indian degrees, compared to the Chinese and

African Asians whose qualifications in the main were from British examination boards and institutions.

The gender contrasts too are important at this level. In all groups, including the Caribbeans, men were much more likely than women to have degrees; Caribbean women, however, were and remain much more likely than men to have higher qualifications. In most, possibly all, groups women have been making remarkable progress. In the Fourth Survey sample, in all South Asian groups 16–24-year-old women were more likely to have a degree than their male peers, but this may have been a distortion in the sample as it is not true for the 1991 Census. It nevertheless does represent a trend of women at least catching up with the high rates of higher education participation among South Asian males. The Chinese seem to be a group which has for some time had gender parity in this respect, and the Caribbeans are the only group among which female participation is greater than among males. For example, admission figures for polytechnics (as they were then called) in 1990 and 1991 show that Caribbean women were 50 per cent more likely than men to be entering those institutions (Modood, 1993: Table 1).

Hence, in respect of educational qualifications, including degrees, whites are now and have been for some time in the middle. Whites may be at the top of the ethnic hierarchy in terms of entry into certain prestigious universities and courses, but they are certainly not best placed in terms of representation in higher education and the possession of degrees. Even in terms of prestigious universities and courses, whites do not enjoy an unambiguous position at the top. For example, in the two most competitive subjects, medicine and law, ethnic minorities are much better represented than whites (Modood and Shiner, 1994). In Chapter 10 of this book, Esmail and Dewart discuss discrimination against ethnic minorities in medical school examinations. At the same time their case study reveals that in the 1994 final year cohort at Manchester Medical School 30 per cent of the men and 20 per cent of women were from ethnic minorities – quite an achievement at the top end of competition from a population forming well under 10 per cent of the age cohort. Moreover, despite consisting of a larger slice of candidates' ethnic minority persons had slightly higher average A-level grades.

PARTICIPATION IN POST-COMPULSORY EDUCATION

The full extent of the ethnic minority drive for qualifications is revealed when we consider the rate of participation in post-compulsory education. The staying-on rates for 16–19-year-old whites, Caribbeans and Pakistani/Bangladeshi women were similar (just under half the age group for men, over half for women), but higher for Indian/African Asian women, and much higher for South Asian men. The proportions drop considerably among 20–24-year-olds, but they drop most for whites, who had a lower participation rate in this age group than the Caribbeans (Caribbean men being two and a half times as likely to be in full-time education at this age as white men). South Asians were most likely to be continuing in education, and in reverse to whites, men more so than women, though Indian/African Asian women were twice and Pakistani/ Bangladeshi women one and a half times as likely to be in full-time study in their early 20s as were white women. No ethnic minority group has a lower participation rate in post-16 education than white people, and some have a much higher rate. The data also suggest that people from ethnic minorities in general are also staying on for longer periods.

Looking at participation by qualification levels shows where the real difference between whites and minorities is. The proportion of this age group who had not achieved a GCSE or equivalent but were still in full-time education was a quarter for whites and a fifth for the minorities collectively. It is when we look at those with a GCSE or higher qualification who were continuing in (or had returned to) full-time education that we see a degree of minority commitment quite different from that of whites. Table 3.2 shows that while among the qualified 16–24-year-old whites, about a quarter were likely to be in full-time education (more for women, less for men), nearly half of the ethnic minority women and well over half of the men were. The commitment to education is manifest in groups that were not particularly well qualified at the time of migration: qualified Caribbeans of both sexes in this cohort were considerably more likely to be in full-time education than their white peers, and the qualified Pakistanis/ Bangladeshis had the highest participation rate for each sex.

Children of parents with higher qualifications normally are more likely to pursue higher qualifications themselves, and so given what we have seen of the migrant generations' qualifications, the higher staying-on rates among some groups is perhaps to be expected. To this might be added the motivational drive for self-improvement that migrants typically have for themselves and their children. Moreover, the presence of high rates of youth unemployment, especially among those without qualifications, and the knowledge that ethnic minorities suffer much higher rates of unemployment, may be

Table 3.2   Proportion of qualified 16–24-year-olds in full-time
             education

cell percentages

	White	Caribbean	Indian/ African- Asian	Pakistani	All ethnic minorities
Has O-level or higher and is in full-time education					
Men	21	34	63	71	58
Women	28	40	47	48	46
Weighted count					
Men	*163*	*105*	*166*	*105*	*413*
Women	*145*	*137*	*187*	*101*	*471*
Unweighted count					
Men	*116*	*48*	*110*	*119*	*293*
Women	*119*	*73*	*124*	*119*	*334*

thought to all add to the explanation of why the ethnic minorities
have high staying-on rates. Operative against these factors may
perhaps only be the negative experience of schooling that some
pupils, especially of working class origins, have, and which some
groups of minorities have, especially Caribbean males (Mac an
Ghaill, 1988). A symptom of the latter is for example evident in the
very high rates of exclusion experienced by Caribbean boys (Gillborn
and Gipps, 1996: 50–53). The evidence is, however, that the ethnic
minority youngsters who do, or who are allowed to, stay on do so for
positive reasons. A study of 16-year-olds in six inner city areas also
found that minority ethnic individuals were more likely to stay on
than whites; of those that stayed on, half wanted to go to university
eventually, while less than a fifth gave as one of their reasons for
staying-on that it was better than being unemployed (Hagell and
Shaw, 1996: 88). Further analysis of that survey shows that Asians
were no more likely than whites, and Caribbeans little more likely, to
say that they stayed on in education because it was better than being
unemployed. On the other hand, ethnic minorities were much more
likely than whites to say that they wanted to improve their
educational qualifications or go to university. The knowledge that
qualifications are necessary for getting a (desirable) job may well
motivate ethnic minorities more than whites, but it seems to do so
positively rather than negatively (see also Basit, 1997 and Wrench
and Qureshi, 1996).

Higher participation rates do not in themselves mean high levels of qualifications and better career prospects. Some of the high level of minority participation in post-compulsory full-time education is likely to be a reflection of the fact that whites, especially white men, are more likely to be in work, and to be pursuing their further education and training while in work, possibly in an apprenticeship or through part-time participation in education (Drew et al, 1992; Drew, 1995; Hagell and Shaw, 1996). A further reason why ethnic minorities are more likely than whites to be in full-time education is that ethnic minorities may on average take longer to achieve their qualifications, or may be more likely to be 'returners' to full-time education. This interpretation seems to be supported by Table 3.3 which shows the age at which those who acquired an A-level or equivalent in the previous decade did so. It is quite clear that ethnic minorities were less likely to acquire that qualification at age 18 or under, were twice as likely as whites to acquire it at age 19, and were slightly more likely to acquire it as a returner or mature student. Some of the lateness in attainment may be due to taking 're-sits' to improve grades or the number of passes, for there is evidence that ethnic minorities have been more likely to obtain their quali-fications in more than one sitting. A special relevance of these differences is where, as for example in university entrance selection, qualifications obtained in more than one sitting are valued less than those obtained in one sitting, to the detriment of ethnic minorities and perhaps risking discrimination (Modood and Shiner, 1994: 29). These two factors, less likelihood of selection for work-based part-time education or training, and late attainment, are, however, unlikely to explain in full the very high levels of ethnic minority participation in post-16 full-time education, especially, as there is evidence from the Fourth Survey that the lateness in attainment may well have been a generational phenomenon and is now disappearing.

Table 3.4 shows that among 16–24-year-olds, some ethnic minority groups are now more likely to obtain all or most of their O-levels at 16 or under than whites. In fact, for most groups there was no real difference between this age cohort and the older cohort of 25-34-year-olds. The one exception were the Caribbeans; only 56 per cent of the older group with O-levels or equivalent acquired most of them at 16 or under, compared to 88 per cent of the younger group, the same rate as their white peers. For other groups, the improve-ment among younger people was relatively slight, and in fact except for the Indians there is little difference between whites and most minority groups in the age at which GCSEs are achieved. Why only

Table 3.3   Age at which A-levels were obtained

column percentages

	White	Caribbean	Indian/ African- Asia	Pakistani/ Bangladeshi	All ethnic minorities
Age					
18 or under	86	(67)	73	66	70
19	8	(16)	13	15	15
20 or over	12	(17)	14	20	16
Weighted count	*107*	*58*	*159*	*60*	*305*
Unweighted count	*94*	*35*	*113*	*56*	*215*

Base: 20–29-year-olds

Figures in parentheses denote small sample sizes.

seven in ten Indians should attain these qualifications by or at age 16, compared to eight in ten or better for all other groups, is not at all clear, except that it was the case that 16–24-year-old Indians without qualifications were more likely than any other group (twice as likely as Pakistanis; four times as likely as Bangladeshis) to be in full-time education. Their slower rate of attainment is therefore an indication of their higher level of participation and persistence; and therefore, of a movement away from the qualifications-polarisation of older Indians, which continues to be a characteristic of the Pakistanis.

Table 3.4   Age at which O-levels were obtained

column percentages

	White	Caribbean	Indian	African- Asian	Pakistani/ Bangladeshi	All ethnic minorities
Age						
16 or under	86	86	72	88	79	80
17	13	12	22	6	14	14
18 or over	1	1	6	7	8	5
Weighted count	*254*	*201*	*198*	*95*	*162*	*728*
Unweighted count	*191*	*101*	*136*	*53*	*178*	*498*

Base: 16–24-year-olds

Given the discussion so far, it should be no surprise that most minority groups are over-represented in higher education. This can

**Table 3.5   Domiciled first year full-time and part-time students
by age group, 1994–95 (proportion of age group from
1991 Census figures given in parentheses)**

column percentages

	18–20 years	21–27 years	28–37 years	38–47 years	48 years and over
Ethnic group					
White	87.8 (92.7)	83.5 (93.1)	86.4 (93.1)	91.8 (94.8)	93.1 (97.3)
Black*	1.7 (1.8)	5.8 (2.1)	7.7 (2.5)	3.7 (1.2)	2.8 (0.9)
Indian**	4.5 (2.0)	3.6 (1.8)	1.4 (1.8)	0.9 (1.8)	1.1 (0.8)
Pakistani	2.0 (1.4)	2.4 (1.1)	0.6 (0.8)	0.4 (0.7)	0.3 (0.3)
Other groups	4.0 (2.1)	4.6 (1.8)	3.9 (1.8)	3.3 (1.5)	2.7 (0.6)

*   'Black' includes black Africans as well as Caribbeans
** 'Indian' includes African-Asians
Source: Higher Education Statistics Agency

be seen in Table 3.5 from the Higher Education Statistics Agency
(HESA), which presents the figures of first year university students
in the year 1994–95 by age group, with a comparison of the
proportion in the age group in the population. It shows, for example,
that twice the proportion of 18–27-year-old Indians entered university as whites. It shows also that the over-representation of black
students is considerable, but only among those aged 21 years or
over. HESA has linked this to the fact that black students form a
larger percentage among part-timers than among full-timers, for
part-time students tend to come from the older age groups (HESA,
1995: 26). Nevertheless, analysis of the data shows that even after
taking academic and social class related factors into account,
significant ethnic differences in the rates of admission remain
unexplained (Modood and Shiner, 1994). The most worrying of these
is that Caribbean and Pakistani applicants were less likely than other
candidates to gain admission to the pre-1992 universities.[2] A follow-
up study by Modood and Shiner is under way to examine to what
extent this is due to discrimination by universities and if variations in
A-level predictions by schools on UCAS forms can account for any of
the ethnic differences in the rates of admissions (details available
from Modood). Moreover, now that ethnic minorities are seen to be a
significant component in higher education (there even are some
institutions where whites are no longer a majority among the student

2   In 1992 the polytechnics, as they then were, became universities. So
'pre-1992 universities' refers to those that were not till recently
polytechnics.

population), there are wider issues about equal opportunities, pedagogy and the multicultural responsibilities of a university (Cohen, 1995). To date, research on ethnicity and educational attainment has concentrated on schools (Gillborn and Gipps, 1996), but it is time for researchers to give more attention to further and higher education.

ETHNIC MINORITY EDUCATIONAL DRIVE

Ethnic minorities, then, have made and are making remarkable educational progress and, despite some exceptions, are well represented in higher education today. Participation and attainment levels among 16–19-year-olds suggest that their share in higher education will grow. In the period of time under consideration, whites too have made progress. Nevertheless, the ethnic minority achievement stands out because of at least three factors. Firstly, it has at least in part bucked the determinants of class: despite their worse parental occupational profile, most minority groups are producing greater proportions of applications and admissions to higher education than the rest of the population. Secondly, most minority groups have had to struggle over the learning of the English language, the acquisition of new cultural reference points and the travails of cultural adaptation and settlement in a new country. Thirdly, all this has had to be achieved in the face of societal racism and, in particular, negative stereotyping, lower expectations and sometimes racial harassment in schools.

What has made this impressive progress possible? Both the characteristics and the circumstances of these groups are relevant. Among group characteristics I would emphasise the economic motivation of migrants, the desire to better themselves and especially the prospects for their children. The belief in the value of education in achieving upward mobility and respectability is related to this, as is the strong academic orientation of most minority groups, not just the South Asians and the Chinese as mentioned above, but also the Africans, who were not included in the Fourth Survey but emerged in the 1991 Census as the group with the highest proportion of persons with higher qualifications (Owen, Mortimore and Phoenix, 1997). The group circumstances I have in mind include the fact that due to racial discrimination migrants often suffered a downward social mobility on entry into Britain (Modood et al, 1997: 141–142). The only jobs open to them were often below their qualification levels and below the social class level they enjoyed before migration. This meant that not only did many value education more than their white workmates but saw it as part of the process of reversing the initial downward mobility, especially in the lives of their children. The continuing presence of racial discrimination has also meant that non-white persons have been particularly dependent on qualifications for jobs and economic progression, especially as they lacked the social networks, such as those associated with Oxbridge or certain working-class occupations, to help them get on. These factors worked together to make qualifications and higher education of more value, of more urgency, to ethnic minority than white people.

While it is important to insist that the experiences and qualification levels vary markedly between minority groups and cannot be homogenised into a single 'black' phenomenon, nevertheless, when we consider some of the obstacles surrounding ethnic minority educational attainment, ethnic minorities have been and are doing better than till recently looked likely to most researchers.

Chapter 4

Black Women in Education: A Collective Movement for Social Change

Heidi Safia Mirza

This chapter is concerned with the issue of how to theorise the paradox of inclusive acts by excluded groups. Research on young black (African-Caribbean) women's strategies to succeed at school and into further and higher education raises the question, 'How can such conservative and instrumental actions be deemed subversive?' On the surface, it appears that they are conforming, identifying with the ideology of meritocracy, climbing the conventional career ladder, wanting to succeed on society's terms – buying into the system. The problem is simply this, how can I claim (as I do) that black women's desire or motivation to succeed within the educational system is radical? How can what appears on the surface to be compliance and willingness to conform to systems and structures of educational meritocracy be redefined as strategic or as evidence of a covert social movement for change?

What we need is a complex analysis of what is going on among the majority of black women who are not, as we have come to expect from the popular presumptions, 'failing'. We need to move toward a coherent understanding of black female educational orientation that begins to reveal the subversive and transformative possibilities of their actions. From school through to university and into the community, black women access educational resources and subvert expected patterns of educational mobility. This active engagement challenges our expectations. Black women who have been, after all, theorised in our dominant academic discourse as 'the most oppressed', deemed the least 'visible', the least empowered, the

Reprinted from Heidi Safia Mirza (1997) (ed) *Black British Feminism: A Reader.* London: Routledge. The editors thank Routledge for permission to reprint.

most marginal of groups, do relatively well. They appear to strive for inclusivity.

However, no one wants to look at their success, their desire for inclusivity. They are out of place, disrupting, untidy. They do not fit. The notion of their agency and difference is problematic for the limited essentialist and mechanical social reproduction theories that dominate our explanations of black female inequality (Moore, 1996). Traditionally, and in commonsense accounts that rely on such theories, black women's contradictory actions are analysed in terms of subcultural resistance.

However, because young black women's subcultures of resistance are deemed conformist, the idea is cleverly reworked and presented instead as 'resistance through accommodation' (Mac an Ghaill, 1988). Black women, we are told, employ this particular strategy of resistance because they are motivated by their identification with the role model of the 'strong black mother'. Such essentialist constructions presume that the role model of the black mother provides young black women with special powers of endurance and transgenerational cultural understandings that especially equip them in their struggles against racism and sexism (Mirza, 1992).

But in this chapter I want to suggest that black female educational urgency cannot be understood simply as 'resistance through accommodation'. Their desire for inclusion is strategic, subversive and ultimately far more transformative than subcultural reproduction theory suggests. The irony is that black women are both succeeding and conforming in order to transform and change. By mapping black women's covert educational urgency I hope to move toward a radical interpretation of black female educational motivation. Valorising their agency as subversive and transformative rather than as a manifestation of resistance, it becomes clear that black women do not just resist racism, they live in 'other' worlds.

EVIDENCE OF COLLECTIVE EDUCATIONAL URGENCY

Black women do buy into the educational system. They do relatively well at school, relative that is to their male and female working class peers as measured in terms of average exam performance at GCSE level. This phenomenon was first documented over 10 years ago in 1985 in the Swann Report and confirmed by the Inner London Education Authority (ILEA) in 1987 (Mirza, 1992). More recently the findings of the National Youth Cohort Study 1992 appear to confirm this (Drew et al, 1992).

In my own research for *Young, Female and Black,* which was a small local study of two inner-city working class schools, I also found black girls do as well, if not better than their peers in average exam performance. I found young black women collectively identified with the notion of credentialism. They subscribed to the meritocratic ideal, which within the parameters of their circumstances meant 'getting on'. In difficult and disruptive conditions the majority of young black women would sit in the back of the class getting on with their own work. However, whatever the young black women's achievements, they were always within the constraints of the class conditions of inner-city schooling.

What is clear from all the studies on race and education is that black girls have to stay on longer at school to achieve their long term educational aspirations. In order to overcome obstacles of racism and sexism in school, large numbers stay on to get the opportunities that enable them to take a 'back door' route into further and higher education. The young women did this by strategically rationalising their educational opportunities. They would opt for accessible careers (gendered and racialised jobs) which would give them the opportunity to get onto a college course. Their career aspirations were tied to their educational motivation and by the prospect of upward mobility. A job was an expression of their desire to move ahead within the educational process. The young black women chose 'realistic careers' that they knew to be accessible and (historically) available to them. For example, social work and other caring jobs such as nursing or office work. The occupations they chose always required a course or several courses of rigorous professional training, and this was why they choose them. Thus while it may appear young black women were reproducing stereotypes of black women's work, they were in effect expressing their meritocratic values within the limits of opportunities allowed to them in a racially and sexually-divisive educational and economic system. They were in effect subversively and collectively employing a back door entry to further and higher education.

This picture of collective educational urgency among young black women to enter colleges of further and higher education is confirmed by national statistics. The 1993 Labour Force survey shows 61 per cent of all black women (aged 16–59) to have higher and other qualifications (*Employment Gazette,* 1993). Figures for 1995 show that 52 per cent of all black women (aged 16–24) are in full-time education, compared to 28 per cent of white women, 36 per cent of black men, and 31 per cent of white men (*Employment Gazette,* 1995). Similarly a recent study for the Policy Studies Institute shows that in relation to their respective population sizes, ethnic minority groups, overall, are over-represented in higher education (Modood and Shiner, 1994). This over-representation was especially apparent in the new universities. Here people of Caribbean origin were over-represented by 43 per cent, Asians by 162 per cent and Africans by 223 per cent. This compared to the white population which was under-represented by 7 per cent.

But educational urgency does not stop there. As mothers, black women strategically negotiate the educational advantage of their children within the constraints offered by decaying urban education system and limited access to cultural capital (Reay, 1998). Black women are disproportionately involved in the setting up and running of black supplementary schools. They invest in the education of the next generation. In ongoing research on black supplementary schools, Diane Reay and myself have conducted a preliminary survey of black schools in London (Reay and Mirza, 1997). So far we found 60 officially documented black schools within four London boroughs, but we believe we only scratched the surface. Through networks and word of mouth we hear of more and more every day. Sometimes there would be several on one council estate. They appear to spring up 'unofficially' in houses, community centres, and unused school rooms. Of those we found, 65 per cent were run by women; and of those run by men, women's involvement as teachers and mentors was the overwhelming majority input.

IS BLACK FEMALE EDUCATIONAL URGENCY A NEW SOCIAL MOVEMENT?

It could be argued, as indeed I wish to suggest here, that the extent, direction and intensity of the black female positive orientation to education is significant enough to qualify their collective action as a transformative social movement. However, Gilroy does not think so. He describes the black struggles for educational opportunities as constituting 'fragile collectivities'. He argues such movements are symptoms of 'resistance to domination', defensive organisations, with their roots in a radical sense of powerlessness. As they cannot make the transition to 'stable forms of politics', they are not agents for social change (Gilroy, 1987: 230–1).

However, I believe an analysis of female collective action offers a new direction in the investigation of black social movements. As Gilroy's argument demonstrates, black female agency has remained invisible in the masculinist discourse of 'race' and social change. There has clearly been a black and male monopoly of the 'black subject' (West, 1990). In the masculinist discourse on race and social change the assumption is that 'race' is contested and fought over in the masculine arena of the streets – among the (male) youth in the city (eg Solomos, 1988; Keith, 1993, 1995; Solomos and Back, 1995). Urban social movements, we are told, mobilise in protest, riots, local politics, and community organisations. It is their action, and not the subversive and covert action of women, that gives rise to so-called 'neo-populist liberatory authentic politics' (Gilroy 1987: 245). This is the masculinist version of radical social change; visible, radical, confrontational, collective action, powerfully expressed in the politics of the inner-city, where class consciousness evolves in response to urban struggle.

Thus notions of resistance which are employed in this male discourse of social change to signify and celebrate black struggle, remain entrenched in ideology that privileges dominance. The black feminist theorist Patricia Hill Collins tells us that black women writers have rejected notions of power based on domination in favour of a notion of power based on a vision of self-actualisation, self-definition and self-determination (Collins, 1991). However, the political language of 'community' around which black social movements are traditionally articulated in the masculinist discourse remains a relational idea. It suggests the notion of antagonism and oppositionality – of domination and subordination – between one community and another (Young, 1990). But what if, for black women, community identity is not relational and antagonistic but inclusive with regard to the mainstream? This could be a possibility; there must be another way of understanding our lives other than always in relation to the 'other'. There is, after all, more to life than opposition to racism (Mirza, 1995).

BLACK WOMEN'S ACTIVISM:
STRATEGIES FOR TRANSFORMATION

Mapping the hidden histories, subjugated knowledges, the counter memories of black women educators in black supplementary schools, reveals the possibilities for covert social movements to achieve social change. Black supplementary schools, as organic grassroots organisations, are not simply a response to mainstream educational exclusion and poor practice, as they are so often described. They are far more radical and subversive than their quiet conformist exterior suggests. It is little wonder they are viewed suspiciously by uninformed observers as 'black power places'. They provide an alternative world with different meaning and shared 'ways of knowing'. As one mother said, 'There is white bias everywhere except at Saturday school.' It is a place where whiteness is displaced and blackness becomes the unspoken norm. It is a place of refusal and difference; a place of belonging.

In the four supplementary schools in our research, black children discovered 'really useful knowledge' (Johnson, 1988) which allowed them 'to step outside the white hermeneutic circle and into the black' (Gates in Casey, 1993: 110). Each of the four schools in our study was distinct, but they were underpinned by two main pedagogies. Some focused more on black images, black history and black role models. Others focused more on back to basics, the formal teaching of the 3 Rs. Some did both.

In the same way as the schools were paradoxically radical and conservative in their aims, so too were the teachers both radical and conservative in their praxis. On the one hand, the women, who were for the most part voluntary unpaid teachers, talked of their 'joy' of what they do, the 'gift of giving back', of their work to 'raise the race'. Many had been giving up their weekends for 20 years. Others had become ill from overwork and dedication. On the other hand the same teachers saw themselves as complementing mainstream education. They were concerned about 'fitting in', assisting parents with home–school relations and getting the children to do better. On the surface these schools appeared conformist and conservative, with their focus on formality and buying into the liberal democratic ideal of meritocracy.

But as Casey writes in her excellent book, *I Answer with My Life,* in a racist society a black person is located very differently than a white person.

> In a racist society for a black child to become educated is to contradict the whole system of racist signification... to succeed in studying white knowledge is to undo the system itself... to refute its reproduction of black inferiority materially and symbolically. (Casey, 1993: 123)

Thus it could be argued that, in certain circumstances, *doing well can become a radical strategy.* An act of social transformation.

Black women educators do not accept the dominant discourse. In their space on the margin they have evolved a system of strategic rationalisation of the dominant discourse. They operate within, between, under and alongside the mainstream educational and labour market structures. Subverting, renaming and reclaiming opportunities for their children through their transformative pedagogy of 'raising the race'. A radical pedagogy, that ironically appears conservative on the surface with its focus on inclusion and dialogue with the mainstream.

Patricia Hill Collins (1991) calls our attention to the dual nature of black women's activist traditions in their attempt to bring about social change. She suggests black women engage in activism that is both conservative and radical. Black women create culture and provide for their families. Fostering self-evaluation and self-reliance, patterns of consciousness and self-expression shape their cultures of difference. This struggle for group survival may appear conservative with its emphasis on preserving customs and cultural maintenance. Collins argues this struggle for group survival is in contrast to the radical tradition of black women's engaged activism. Because black communities and families are so profoundly affected by the political economic and social institutions they are situated in, black women also find themselves working for radical institutional transformation through legal and civil action in terms of the traditional and valorised (masculine) form of visible social action.

However it is in the uncharted struggle for group survival that black women in supplementary schools are located. Rose, a mother in one of the schools, tells us:

> We always have a session which is about giving children a voice. We teach them to speak, to develop a voice that can be heard. We tell them to be proud of what they are, to be strong about speaking out. I think perhaps that is the most important thing we do, helping them develop a voice that gets heard because it is easy for black children not to be listened to in school, to be thought of as a nuisance when they say something. I think in Saturday school it is quite clear that they are expected, entitled to speak out. (Rose: in Reay and Mirza, 1997)

Charity's narrative on how Colibri was started includes similar themes of activism, community and commitment that characterise the struggle for group survival and the desire for social change:

> There was a group of about six parents who, like myself as a black teacher, were dissatisfied with what was happening to black pupils. They felt if they had been in the Caribbean their children would be

much further on academically and they decided something had to be done, schools weren't doing anything, so it had to be them. I really wish someone had the time to chart the enormous amount of work they put in those first few years. It was immense. The school started off in someone's front room on Saturday mornings. The parents doing all the teaching themselves to start with and it was very much focused on what was their main concern; their children not being able to read and write properly. Then these parents found the group of children grew from 10 to 15 and soon it was 20 and at this point it was unmanageable running a Saturday school in someone's front room so they petitioned the council for accommodation and finally got one of the council's derelict properties. They spent their spare time shovelling rubbish out of the room, tramps had been living there. Doing building, repair work, getting groups of parents together to decorate. They pulled together and did all this work themselves, used the expertise they had to get the school on its feet. (Charity: in Reay and Mirza, 1997)

What the black women appeared to have learnt is an awareness of the need for social support and collaborative action through their experience of marginality in a white racist society. From this awakening of consciousness and socio-analysis (Bourdieu, 1990: 116) the women created their own cultural capital. Their habitus embodied 'real intelligence' in their ways of knowing and understanding (Luttrell, 1992). As their words show, this ultimately led to collective action and social change.

CONCLUSION

In conclusion, the question we must return to is this: 'Is the coherent educational urgency uncovered among black women a radical social movement with transformative possibilities from the margin, or as some suggest no more than a conservative act?'

Research on black women in education shows there is much evidence to suggest black women do not accept the dominant discourse, nor do they construct their identities in opposition to the dominant discourse. They redefine the world, have their own values, codes and understandings, *refuse* (not resist) the gaze of the other. As Spivak says: 'Marginal groups do not wish to claim centrality but redefine the big word human in terms of the marginal' (quoted in hooks, 1991: 22). Black women live in counter-hegemonic marginal spaces where, as hooks describes: 'Radical black subjectivity is seen not overseen by any authoritative other claiming to know us better than we know ourselves' (hooks, 1991: 22).

For black women, strategies for everyday survival consist of trying to create spheres of influence that are separate from but engaged with existing structures of oppression. Being successful and gaining authority and power within institutions that have traditionally not allowed black women formal authority or real power enables them to indirectly subvert oppressive structures by changing them. By saying this I do not wish to argue that black women are simply empowered through their educational achievement. Empowerment assumes a notion of power that is relational. It suggests the positive power of a collectivity or individual to challenge basic power relations in society (Yuval-Davis, 1994). The assumption is that black women's actions empower them, but any gains are always oppositional and in relation to the hegemonic culture (Steady, 1993). What I have tried to show instead is that black women are not simply resisting, but have evolved a system of strategic rationalisation which has its own logic, values and codes. Black women struggle for educational inclusion in order to transform their opportunities and so in the process subvert racist expectations and beliefs. By entering into dialogue with others, they are not conservative or colluding with the mainstream. They are collectively opening up transformative possibilities for their community through their pragmatic recognition of the power of education to transform and change the hegemonic discourse (McLaren, 1994; hooks, 1994).

So, finally, may I claim black women's educational urgency and desire to do well within the system is radical and subversive? To answer the question I leave you with the words of a black woman university student:

When not given success we need to be successful... that is the most radical thing you can do. (Alisha: in Mirza, 1994)

Part Two

Negotiating Access to Higher Education

Chapter 5

What Are Ethnic Minorities Looking For?[1]

Alison Allen

This chapter is based upon a research project conducted by Heist in 1995 and looks at three issues regarding the pre-higher education decision-making process. First it examines the influences on ethnic minority and white students when deciding to enter higher education. Secondly, the chapter explores the reasons why students choose to apply to particular higher education institutions. Finally, a comparison is made of ethnic minority and white students' motives for selecting their current subject of study. In addressing these issues the analysis pays particular attention to the role of the family and of those professionals in contact with students in order to ascertain their influence on students' decision-making prior to university entry.

SURVEY METHODS

The main part of the research project comprised a postal questionnaire of full-time ethnic minority undergraduates and, for comparative purposes, some white undergraduates in British universities in May 1995. The response rate for the 1,900 questionnaires distributed was disappointing, particularly for ethnic minority students. For ethnic minority students only 147 responses were received, with 91 responses for white students (10 per cent and 19 per cent response rates, respectively). As Table 5.1 demonstrates, the sample of ethnic minority students also over-

1 The author wishes to acknowledge Heist, who conducted the research upon which this chapter is based, together with the author and her co-editor of the final publication, *Higher Education: The Ethnic Minority Experience*, Ebrahim Adia and Dave Roberts.

represented the Chinese and Indian groups and under-represented
the Bangladeshi and black groups. For these reasons, caution should
be exercised when interpreting the project findings.

**Table 5.1   Comparison of Heist achieved sample with UK
              higher education admissions**

percentages

	Respondents	UK ethnic minority 1992 admissions (under 25)*
Indian	37	29.6
Chinese	20	5.8
Pakistani	19	18.8
Bangladeshi	3	6.8
Black Caribbean	13} (21)	16.9}
Black African	8}	7.9} (32.6)
Black Other		7.8}
Other		6.5
Total	100	100.1

* Source: Modood and Shiner (1994)

A small number of in-depth interviews and focus group discussions
were conducted before the main survey to assist in the
questionnaire design. Follow-up interviews were later conducted to
explore some of the survey findings.

THE FAMILY AND ITS PERCEPTION OF HIGHER EDUCATION

The preliminary qualitative research revealed that irrespective of the
social class and cultural background of ethnic minority students, the
general consensus was that the family is very encouraging, proud
and supportive of ethnic minority students' plans to go on to higher
education. A typical comment:

> My parents encouraged me to go to HE because they didn't have the
> opportunity, having to bring up a family, having to work. There is a lot of
> support from them seeing me go to university.

Students with middle class parents/guardians said that going on to
higher education was taken for granted and there was never an
alternative. Indeed a number of students felt that family expectations

could be so great that they were almost being pressurised into higher education. It was suggested that male students may receive greater encouragement or in turn feel more pressurised.

In the questionnaire survey, respondents were asked to indicate the extent to which they agreed or disagreed with the statement, 'Higher education is greatly valued by my family'. Table 5.2 shows that a higher proportion of ethnic minority respondents agreed (84 per cent) with the statement than whites (55 per cent). There were no significant differences in the responses given in terms of social background of respondents (occupation of the main wage earner in their household).

Such overwhelming support for higher education among ethnic minority families can inter alia be explained by the point made by Modood (1993) that some ethnic minorities use higher education to alter their class composition and Singh's (1990) comment:

> Parents [in ethnic minority communities] who encourage their children to aspire to achieve the maximum level of education, earn recognition, pride, status within their own community... In the case of Asian girls, higher educational qualifications are thought to improve considerably their chance in the 'marriage market'.

Table 5.2   Higher education is greatly valued by my family

column percentages

	White	Ethnic minority
Strongly agree	18	58
Agree	37	26
Neither agree nor disagree	34	11
Disagree	4	1
Strongly disagree	6	4

HIGHER EDUCATION AND PARENTAL ASPIRATIONS

Given the above finding, it is not surprising that 71 per cent of ethnic minority respondents either agreed or strongly agreed that their parents/guardians wanted all their children to go to university. Only 36 per cent of white respondents agreed or strongly agreed with the proposition (see Table 5.3). This suggests that the higher education institutions should have a strategy for targeting existing and past students' siblings, particularly for ethnic minority students.

Table 5.3　**My parents/guardians wanted all their children to go to university**

	column percentages	
	White	Ethnic minority
Strongly agree	14	48
Agree	22	23
Neither agree nor disagree	33	17
Disagree	25	9
Strongly disagree	6	3

HIGHER EDUCATION AND FAMILY TRADITION

Although a higher proportion of ethnic minority students said higher education was greatly valued by their family, this was not due to a stronger family tradition of higher education study. 59 per cent of ethnic minority students knew of an immediate family member (mother, father, brother or sister) who had studied at a university or college of higher education in the UK, compared with 63 per cent of white students (see Table 5.4). 19 per cent of ethnic minority students had immediate family members who had been educated at an institution abroad, compared with only 3 per cent of white students. 34 per cent of ethnic minority and 36 per cent of white students were first generation higher education students.

Table 5.4　**Has any member of your immediate family ever been educated at a university or college of higher education?**

	column percentages	
	White	Ethnic minority
Yes – at the same institution	2	6
Yes – at another institution in the UK	61	48
Yes – at an institution abroad	3	17
No	36	31

FAMILY ENCOURAGEMENT TO UNDERTAKE HIGHER EDUCATION STUDY

Not surprisingly, given the high proportion of ethnic minority students who said their family had greatly valued higher education,

88 per cent of ethnic minority students said their family had either strongly encouraged or encouraged them to enter higher education (see Table 5.5), compared with 78 per cent of white respondents. Only 2 per cent of ethnic minority and 3 per cent of white respondents said their family had discouraged them.

Table 5.5   Extent of family encouragement to enter higher education

		column percentages
	White	Ethnic minority
Strongly encouraged	34	55
Encouraged	44	33
Neither encouraged nor discouraged	19	10
Discouraged	3	1
Strongly discouraged	–	1

Respondents who had been 'strongly encouraged' to enter higher education were asked to explain the reason/s for their answer. Over half of ethnic minority respondents (54 per cent) and nearly a third of white respondents (32 per cent) who had been 'strongly encouraged' by their families exposed the reasons for such strong encouragement.

Improved job prospects and aspiring to a better future were the main reasons given by both ethnic minority and white respondents. This confirms Modood's (1993) assertion that some ethnic minority groups use higher education to ascend social classes. Other reasons given by respondents in this survey included following a family tradition and improving on parents' economic/social position. Ethnic minority respondents also made reference to family pride being enhanced by family members obtaining a higher education qualification. This supports Singh's (1990) reasoning that parents of Asian families assume higher status within the community commensurate with the qualifications procured by their children.

Inter alia, several white respondents maintained that family encouragement was a corollary of the fact that they had expressed a desire to take a higher education course. Statements of this nature were conspicuous by their absence from ethnic minority respondents, many of whom appeared to have been offered little alternative but to enter higher education.

Comments from ethnic minority students who had been strongly encouraged to enter higher education:

> My parents expected all of us to go to university, there was not really an option.

> They (parents) feel it will be better for my future career, as it's easier to get a job.

> Sons/daughters of my parents' friends have studied at university and have respectable jobs.

> They wanted me to succeed in life generally and an education is the only way to do it.

> It is important in my family to get a good degree as then you get a more educated husband too!

> My parents are both highly educated and know the importance of higher education.

> I was pressured into entering higher education but it is the one way of gaining status in the Chinese community.

Comments from white students who had been strongly encouraged to enter higher education included:

> Because they didn't go and now regret it. They basically want me to do it for them.

> My mum went back into education in her 40s and regretted not getting a degree earlier so she has encouraged me while I am still young.

> Because they knew it was what I wanted and therefore they encouraged me to achieve it.

> All my family have been to university.

ENCOURAGEMENT FOR GIRLS TO ENTER HIGHER EDUCATION

In response to the statement 'In my culture girls are not encouraged to enter higher education as much as boys', 14 per cent of ethnic minority and 31 per cent of white respondents considered the statement 'not applicable'. Of those who did think the statement was applicable, ethnic minority students were more likely to agree with the statement (20 per cent) than white students (8 per cent) (see Table 5.6). There were no significant differences in the responses of males compared with females. Among ethnic minority students, Pakistani, Bangladeshi and Indian respondents were most likely to agree with the statement. This suggests there is a greater tendency in South East Asian cultures to encourage boys to enter higher education.

Table 5.6   In my culture girls are not encouraged to enter higher education as much as boys

		column percentages
	White	Ethnic minority
Strongly agree	3	7
Agree	5	13
Neither agree nor disagree	8	18
Disagree	25	23
Strongly disagree	59	39

INFLUENCES UPON DECISION TO ENTER HIGHER EDUCATION

This section attempts to establish the relative influence of different family members and professionals upon respondents' decision to enter higher education. Respondents were asked to rate the importance of various family members and professionals in their decision to enter higher education. The results are shown in Table 5.7.

Influence of parents/guardians

The preliminary qualitative research revealed that parents had played an important part in ethnic minority students' decision to go on to higher education. A typical comment was:

> My father encouraged me to go onto higher education, so did my mother. They think that education is the best thing. I have three brothers and four sisters. My brothers had been to HE.

Education is highly valued in Asian, Chinese and African cultures. Some students felt that they were given no choice. For example, one Afro-Caribbean student commented:

> My parents decided that I had to go to university, otherwise I'd be kicked out of the house, either university or out. All my brothers and sisters have been to university. We have no choice at all.

As Table 5.7 shows, ethnic minority students were much more likely to rate the influence of their female parent/guardian as 'very important' in their decision to enter higher education (38 per cent), compared with only 14 per cent of white students. 47 per cent of whites considered the influence of their mother/female guardian as 'important' compared with 38 per cent of ethnic minority students.

For both ethnic minority and white respondents, the father/male guardian also exercised considerable influence, but slightly less than their female counterparts. 70 per cent of ethnic minority and 58 per cent of white students, said their father/male guardian had exercised either an 'important' or 'very important' role.

Influence of other relatives

A smaller proportion of ethnic minority and white respondents rated the influence of other relatives as an important influence, but again their influence was more pronounced amongst ethnic minority respondents. 15 per cent compared to only 1 per cent of white respondents felt that relatives other than their mother/father or male/female guardian had played a 'very important' role in their decision to enter higher education. A further 31 per cent of ethnic minority respondents and 21 per cent of white respondents classified the influence of other relatives as 'important'.

Influence of careers advisors

Similar proportions of ethnic minority (43 per cent) and white respondents (44 per cent) said they had discussed their career/ higher education plans with a careers advisor prior to starting their current course. However, a disturbingly high proportion of all respondents (57 per cent ethnic minority and 56 per cent white) said they had not done so. Mature students were less likely to have consulted careers advisors. 50 per cent of white and 51 per cent of ethnic minority respondents who were under 21 years old at the time of enrolling on their current course said they had discussed their plans with a careers advisor compared with 30 per cent of white and 23 per cent of ethnic minority students 21 years or older.

The fact that relatively few respondents had consulted careers advisors is out of line with findings from unpublished research undertaken by Heist for consultancy clients. In a recent survey of over 500 traditional 18-year-old applicants (a significant number of whom were ethnic minority students), nearly four out of five said they had discussed their higher education course with a careers

Table 5.7 Influence on decision to enter higher education

cell percentages

	Not at all important		Not important		Neither important nor unimportant		Important		Very important	
	Ethnic minorities	White	Ethnic minorities	White	Ethnic minorities	White	Ethnic minorities	White	Ethnic minorities	White
Mother/female guardian	6	7	1	5	17	28	38	47	38	14
Father/male guardian	8	12	6	6	15	25	37	46	33	12
Other relatives	17	28	11	12	26	38	31	21	15	1
Careers advisers	20	30	16	16	32	30	27	21	5	2
School teachers	15	26	9	7	34	27	26	33	15	7
Friends	13	18	10	7	32	33	29	33	16	9

teacher. Table 5.7 shows that only 32 per cent of ethnic minority and 23 per cent of white respondents in this survey rated the influence of careers advisers as important in their decision-making.

Clearly those respondents who had discussed their career/higher education plans with a careers advisor prior to starting their current course were more likely to rate the influence of careers advisors as being important in their decision to enter higher education. 40 per cent of white and 48 per cent of ethnic minority respondents who had discussed their plans with a careers advisor said careers advisors were either a ' very important' or 'important' influence.

A small-scale research study carried out at four UK universities (Rahme, 1995) revealed that in 70 per cent of cases, careers advice given to higher education students of ethnic minority origin at each stage of their education, (when aged between 11–16, 16–18, 18–21 and 21+) decreased their confidence and motivation. There was evidence of careers advisors lowering the ambitions of high academic achievers of ethnic minority origin by suggesting less demanding courses. Unfortunately, no comparisons with white students were made.

In this survey respondents who had discussed their career/higher education plans with careers advisors prior to starting their current course were asked to list any comments regarding the advice given to them and if the advisors had suggested any alternative careers. There was no evidence of significant differences in the advice given to ethnic minority and white respondents. A high percentage of ethnic minority (39 per cent) and white respondents (33 per cent) who had approached a careers advisor claimed the careers service had *not* been useful, that they had been unhelpful or had discouraged them from entering higher education. We do not of course know how realistic the students' career/higher education plans were.

Comments provided by ethnic minority students in this survey regarding the careers advice received included:

Was very sketchy, not detailed or organised enough, did not give me any alternatives.

They were pretty useless and I did most of the work myself.

Was discouraged from entering higher education.

Suggested I get a full time job as soon as possible.

Very, very unhelpful.

Encouraging/informative.

> She supported my decision and had every confidence in me to perform.

> They were excellent, but it was never made clear that that not going on to higher education was actually possible.

Comments from white students included:

> To set a goal and then try to achieve it, they encouraged me to follow my instincts/gave me a list of institutions.

> They told me not to do the degree because I would not pass. I ignored them and no other option was offered.

> I wasn't going on to university, but due to my GCSE results I was strongly encouraged to come.

> Not really useful – they said do what you want to do and go for it.

> They said because I did not have A-levels I would have trouble getting into higher education. They discouraged me and made me feel incompetent. They were very unhelpful.

Influence of school teachers

41 per cent of ethnic minority and 40 per cent of white respondents regarded school teachers as having an 'important' or 'very important' influence on their decision to enter higher education. Slightly fewer ethnic minority than white respondents (24 per cent compared to 33 per cent) considered the influence of school teachers as either 'not important' or 'not at all important'.

Influence of friends

Friends were an important influence on all respondents in their decision to enter higher education. 45 per cent of ethnic minority and 42 per cent of white respondents assessed the influence of friends as either 'important' or 'very important'.

WHY TAKE A HIGHER EDUCATION COURSE?

There was strong evidence in the preliminary qualitative research that ethnic minority students were highly motivated to enter higher education and to achieve academically. The majority of students, irrespective of whether they had worked before or not, had gone into higher education in the hope of better job prospects. They felt that they had to have at least a degree or more in order to achieve anything. One black mature student was keen to share her experience:

Having worked for a number of companies here, you need qualifications and you really need to excel if you are from an ethnic minority. For example, I was working as a secretary at a bank and I had all of the qualifications as a secretary. There was an administrative secretary at the bank and she had to leave. There was another girl who did not have as good qualifications as I had, but because I was black, they did not put me there. That caused me a lot of frustration, so I decided that I'd get more qualifications or as much as I can, and then I'll be able to fight more.

Not everyone had such negative experiences. Some students simply felt the thirst to learn. Many wanted to gain entry into a career and going into higher education was seen as the first step. Some felt that university/college was the place to gain broader knowledge and they would have a sense of achievement if they succeeded:

I chose accountancy because it can lead me somewhere. It can take me up and I can climb the social ladder. I can have a family and money in my pocket and live a comfortable life. At the end of the day that is what I am here for.

The students felt that qualifications were more important for ethnic minority people than their white counterparts as they felt that ethnic minority students were at a disadvantage, particularly in the job market. Ethnic minority students had to be one step ahead of white students in order to compete.

In the questionnaire survey, respondents were asked in an open question to say why they had decided to take a higher education course. The overwhelming reason given by ethnic minority respondents (and among the majority of white respondents) was to secure the job they wanted, and as a variation on the theme, get a better paid job, obtain employment and secure a better future. In short, the majority of respondents perceived higher education as the key to future economic success. This suggests the reason for families encouraging respondents to enter higher education, and the reasons cited by respondents for undertaking a higher education course were consistent.

In addition, a small proportion of ethnic minority and a more significant proportion of white respondents, outlined other reasons for taking a higher education course; namely to avoid employment, enjoy student life, satisfy a yearning to learn and to develop as a person. A higher proportion of ethnic minority than white respondents said they entered higher education due to family pressure or to satisfy family aspirations. This is not surprising given the earlier finding (see Table 5.5) that 88 per cent of ethnic minority students said their family had 'strongly encouraged' or 'encouraged' them to enter higher education.

Examples of ethnic minority respondents' rationale for taking a higher education course included:

> I enjoy studying. I wanted to continue.

> Basically because of family expectations.

> I wanted to further myself and do something I enjoyed, and better myself and not have to struggle like my parents.

> Not ready for employment, not experienced enough for employment. I wanted a degree, not to be a qualified professional.

> It seems a natural progression to go to university after an FE college.

> I want to be properly qualified, being a woman/ethnic has enough drawbacks without ignorance to go with it.

White respondents' reasons included:

> I was expected to by my school/parents and also I did not know what else to do.

> Because I realise you need qualifications to get anywhere and also because I enjoy the subject and the social life.

> I wanted to further my knowledge of various subjects, also I wanted to get away from home.

> It was a natural progression. I did not want to start looking for a job so soon.

> Mid-life change of career/life.

> I had always expected to go to university and so did everyone else around me and I was not ready to start a career at 18.

FACTORS TO BE TAKEN INTO CONSIDERATION DURING INSTITUTION SELECTION

In the questionnaire survey respondents were asked to rate the importance of a range of factors in their decision to attend their current institution as follows:

The academic reputation of the institution

Whilst reputation is 'illusive', there was little difference in ethnic minority and white students' views as to the importance of an institution's academic reputation (see Table 5.8). 18 per cent of ethnic minority respondents regarded the academic reputation as 'very important' and 41 per cent as 'important'. The corresponding figures for white respondents were 14 per cent and 41 per cent respectively. 71 per cent of ethnic minority and 67 per cent of white respondents who were studying at established universities said the academic reputation of the institution was either 'very important' or 'important' to them, compared with 51 per cent of both ethnic minority and white respondents studying at new universities and 48 per cent of ethnic minority and 56 per cent of white students studying at colleges of higher education.

Distance from home

Table 5.8 shows that the distance of higher education institutions from respondents' homes was a significant variable in the decision-making process for 54 per cent of ethnic minority respondents and 47 per cent of white respondents. Taylor (1992) maintains that, in the case of ethnic minority students, if support mechanisms appear to be lacking, 'as suggested by prospectuses, then applying locally and staying near existing methods of support may be an inevitable outcome for some ethnic minority applicants'.

A higher proportion of students studying at institutions less than 21 miles from home said distance from home was an important factor in their decision-making than those who lived some considerable distance away. 77 per cent of ethnic minority and 67 per cent of white respondents who lived less than 21 miles from home said distance from home was either an 'important' or 'very important' factor compared with 35 per cent of ethnic minority and 37 per cent of white respondents who lived more than 120 miles away.

Know someone who is studying/has studied at the institution

To know someone who is studying/has studied at their institution was an important factor for both ethnic minority (25 per cent) and white respondents (20 per cent). Clearly, whether or not respondents did know someone will have influenced their response to this question.

Table 5.8 Influence on choice of higher education institution

cell percentages

	Not at all important		Not important		Neither important nor unimportant		Important		Very important	
	Ethnic minorities	White	Ethnic minorities	White	Ethnic minorities	White	Ethnic minorities	White	Ethnic minorities	White
Academic reputation of the institution	8	8	7	11	26	26	41	41	18	14
Distance from home	10	11	15	16	21	27	36	31	18	16
Knowing someone who is studying/has studied at the institution	33	38	15	16	27	26	21	16	4	4
Cost of living in the locality of the institution	17	23	14	11	36	33	27	24	6	8
Attractive/informative prospectus	9	14	6	4	35	36	40	42	10	3
Entry grade requirements	7	11	4	9	15	20	51	46	23	14
Course content	2	4	-	3	6	4	47	46	45	42
Good social life or outdoor activities	21	12	11	11	27	25	34	40	6	12
High proportion of ethnic minority students in general	31	32	15	16	36	44	11	3	6	4
High proportion of students from own ethnic group	34	33	14	19	43	42	6	5	3	1

The cost of living in the locality of the institution

Table 5.8 shows that there was little difference in the importance attached to the cost of living in the locality of the higher education institutions by ethnic minority and white students. 33 per cent of ethnic minority and 32 per cent of white respondents regarded the cost of living in the locality of the institution as 'important' or 'very important'.

Attractive /informative prospectus

A surprisingly high proportion of both ethnic minority (50 per cent) and white (45 per cent) respondents acknowledged that an attractive/informative prospectus had been an important factor in institution-selection.

Entry grade requirements

Entry grade requirements played a central role in the decision-making of 60 per cent of white and 74 per cent of ethnic minority students during institution selection (see Table 5.8).What we do not know is how many of these students went through Clearing.

Course content

92 per cent of ethnic minority respondents and 88 per cent of white students assessed the course content to be 'important' or 'very important' in their decision-making. This was also evident from the follow-up in-depth interviews:

> I did not bother to see how many black students there were but went for the course.

> The main reason I came was because they were doing Islam within the teacher training within the BEd.

> Good social life or outdoor activities

A good social life or outdoor activities was a greater influence on white students in their choice of institution. As Table 5.8 shows, 52 per cent of white, compared with 40 per cent of ethnic minority respondents, judged this factor to be either 'very important' or 'important' in their selection.

High proportion of ethnic minority students in general

17 per cent of ethnic minority respondents, compared with 7 per cent of whites, considered a high proportion of ethnic minority students at their current institution an 'important' or 'very important' constituent during institution selection. Whilst it is not surprising that a higher proportion of ethnic minority students attached importance to this factor, it was, nonetheless, important to less than one in five ethnic minority students. One possible explanation for this low proportion may be that respondents did not want to admit that this was an important variable. According to Taylor (1992), the tendency among ethnic minorities to apply to institutions which they know have a high proportion of ethnic minority students is largely a function of other institutions presenting a largely 'white' image. Clearly the image of certain locations, eg Bradford, Leicester, may also influence ethnic minority students' applications.

High proportion of students from own ethnic group

Very few white (6 per cent) and ethnic minority respondents (9 per cent) considered a high proportion of students from their own ethnic group as either 'important' or 'very important' in their decision to study at their current institution (see Table 5.8). Half of all ethnic minority (48 per cent) and white respondents (52 per cent) regarded a flourishing presence of students from their own ethnic group as unimportant.

Whilst only a small minority of ethnic minority respondents considered the ethnic balance of their institution an important factor during the institution-selection process, on arrival at their university/college, some valued the presence of students from an ethnic minority background. During the follow-up interviews one student remarked:

> When I first came to [my institution] there were obviously a lot of Asians within the college and that made me feel a bit more settled down to be quite honest... you can identify with Asians, you've got more in common... that made me more relaxed.

She further added:

> I think it's this thing about identifying with your own kind... people tend to have more in common... I am guilty of that because I find I have more in common with Muslim students than with non-Muslim students.

Another student maintained it was:

> Much more comfortable to be with your own people.

REASONS FOR SELECTING CURRENT INSTITUTION

The preliminary qualitative research revealed that, to some extent, parents tried to influence the decision as to which institution ethnic minority students should attend. Some set high expectations for their children to compete for prestigious universities, others wanted their children to go to local institutions. One department head in a higher education college told the researcher that he received a lot of letters from parents, requesting places for their daughters because they did not want them to be away from home.

A number of students had not achieved high enough grades to gain entry to their chosen institution. Particular courses also limited some students' selection. One student chose a course which was only available in London and another institution in Northern Ireland. As she had lived in London for five years, she chose to go to Northern Ireland for a change.

A number of students chose their institution or the course so they could leave home. Some were attracted by the reputation of the student life in a particular location. One Chinese girl commented:

> I wanted to experience life up north as I came from down south.

In the questionnaire survey, respondents were asked in an open question to state the *one* main reason why they had chosen their current institution. Reasons cited by ethnic minority respondents inter alia included the fact that they had achieved the requisite grade requirements, no other institution would accept them and because their current institution was close to home. Several ethnic minority respondents were enticed by the course content and the reputation of the course. Similarly, the course content, the location of the institution, and the fact that it was the only one that would accept them featured as prominent reasons among the white sample. On the whole, ethnic minority respondents placed greater emphasis than white respondents on the proximity and reputation of their present institution.

Ethnic minority respondents' reasons for the selection of their institution included:

Rejected by all other universities, therefore no choice.

I made the grade requirements.

Proximity of home.

The course content.

A combination of bad A-level grades and an attractive/informative campus.

Cost of living cheaper in the Midlands.

My course includes a year abroad in America.

Beautiful campus.

White respondents' reasons included:

I like the place and surroundings.

Only place where they would accept me to do what I aspired as a profession.

Course content.

I could not obtain a large enough grant to afford to live away from home.

A friend had enjoyed his time there and he said that if I went through Clearing that I should ring up.

Reputation it had for good grades.

SOURCES OF INFORMATION DURING INSTITUTION-SELECTION

There was only a marginal difference in the sources used by ethnic minority and white respondents in order to find out about their current institution (see Table 5.9). The most popular source of information, the institution's prospectus or handbook, was consulted by a similar percentage of ethnic minority (66 per cent) and white respondents (64 per cent). 57 per cent of ethnic minority and 60 per cent of white respondents had referred to UCAS/UCCA/PCAS/ADAR directories.

The family was a source of information for a higher proportion of ethnic minority (18 per cent) than white respondents (6 per cent). Although, as shown in Table 5.7, the family was prominent in influencing respondents' decision to enter higher education, it exercised less influence on respondents during institution selection. Most respondents relied upon printed information, friends and the media.

Table 5.9   **Sources of information about current institution**

cell percentages

	White	Ethnic minority
Prospectus/handbook	64	66
UCAS/UCCA/PCAS/ADAR directories	60	57
Career teachers/advisors	28	34
General course directory	26	31
Friends	16	25
Open day	22	19
Careers fairs/exhibition	17	11
Media	13	12
At an interview	6	9
Subject teacher	3	9
Other family members	2	9
Father/male guardian	2	7
Database	5	4
HE magazine/journals	2	6
Mother/female guardian	2	2
School head/principal	2	2
Form/house master/mistress	1	–
Through my employer	1	–
Video	–	1
Base:	*86*	*140*

THE PROSPECTUS COVER

In order to identify whether or not the institution's prospectus cover could have misled respondents into assuming that their institution had a significant ethnic minority student body, the covers of 12 institutions' prospectuses were examined. The institutions were selected on the basis of high, low and average numbers of ethnic minority students. Among the six institutions with high numbers, little attempt was made to portray themselves as multi-ethnic. Only two institutions embodied students from ethnic minority groups on the prospectus cover. The remaining covers either pictured only white students or a building, abstract, etc. Of the two institutions with an average ethnic minority student body, one elected not to display a recognisable face on their prospectus cover, whilst the second showed a female student of mixed origin. Three of the four institutions with a proportionally small ethnic minority student body did not show minority ethnic students on their prospectus covers. One showed both an Asian and a black student.

REASONS FOR CHOOSING CURRENT SUBJECT

The preliminary qualitative research revealed that parents also tried to influence ethnic minority students' decision as to which course to take. Parental preference for accepted professional subjects was a common element in many responses:

> I wanted to do something which is both arts and science, architecture was ideal. My parents wanted me to do medicine. In the African and Indian society, doctor or medicine man is equivalent or close to God. Maybe that's the exaggerated reason, but that is the case. I didn't want to do that, because everybody knew I was doing medicine. So this is the next best thing and my parents accepted it. But they think if you want to do architecture, go to Oxford, Cambridge, Harvard or Princeton. Why here? So I chose it myself.

> I was a computer expert but I did not want to do computers. This course here mixes with all sorts of things, computers, electronics, media, etc. It was my choice. My parents wanted me to be a doctor, or do business. They wanted us to be doctors or lawyers.

> The reason for interior design was because I have always been good at art and design subjects, so I chose it. My parents would prefer me to do something more academic, like medicine or business, etc.

There was a feeling that although many parents wanted their children to take courses in subjects such as medicine, law or business studies, their understanding of higher education institutions and courses was limited, as the majority had not been to higher education themselves. As a result, they could not provide adequate advice or support in their offspring's decision-making process. These students felt that white middle class students would receive more support in terms of advice and information and were, therefore, better prepared for the transfer from school to higher education.

In the questionnaire survey, respondents were given a list of possible reasons for selecting their current subject of study and asked to indicate which, if any, applied to them. As Table 5.10 shows, interest in the course registered as the most popular reason among both ethnic minority (82 per cent) and white respondents (76 per cent), while just over half of all respondents indicated that their current course was a means of obtaining a good job in the future. 38 per cent of the ethnic minority and 41 per cent of the white sample chose their current subject as a prerequisite to entering their chosen career. This confirms the findings listed above that many students were consciously using higher education to either improve their employment prospects or secure a career in their chosen field. Only 1 per cent of ethnic minority and no white respondents said their family chose the subject for them.

12 per cent of ethnic minority but only 2 per cent of white respondents were unable to study the subject of their choice. This may be reflective of the high aspirations of ethnic minority respondents and their families and their attempts to apply for subjects with high entry grades. If this is the case, it is imperative that the guidance process is improved to dissuade prospective students and their families from entertaining unrealistic goals. However, as the findings above show, this may well be seen as discouraging potential applicants from applying to higher education.

Table 5.10 Reasons for choosing current subject

		cell percentages
	White	Ethnic minority
Particular interest in the course	76	82
It will allow me to get a good job in the future	53	54
As a means of entering my chosen career	41	38
As a preliminary to studying for a further qualification	13	22
Couldn't study the subject I wanted – next best	2	12
Only course I could gain entry to	8	6
My family chose it for me	–	1
Funding available from sponsor	1	1
Base:	*90*	*145*

17 per cent of ethnic minority and 16 per cent of white respondents described what subject they would have preferred to have studied and why. The most popular preferred subjects among ethnic minority respondents were medicine, followed by law and business studies/economics. A diverse range of subjects was listed by white respondents.

Choice of subject did appear to be influenced to some extent by family tradition of study in the chosen area, irrespective of ethnic background. 18 per cent of both ethnic minority and white respondents were studying the same subject area as taken by a family member.

SUMMARY

84 per cent of ethnic minority students said higher education is greatly valued by their family compared with 55 per cent of white students.

Ethnic minority families were more likely to encourage their offspring to go on to higher education. 71 per cent compared with 36 per cent of white respondents agreed that their parents/guardians wanted *all* their children to go to university.

Only a third of all respondents did not know of an immediate family member who had been educated at a higher education institution, either in the UK or overseas.

A higher proportion of both ethnic minority and white respondents rated the influence of parents/guardians as important in their decision to enter higher education than other relatives, careers advisors, school teachers or friends. A higher proportion of ethnic minority respondents were more likely to rate the influence of each of these individuals as either 'very important' or 'important' than white students. Family members were also more likely to be sources of information about their current institution for ethnic minority students.

A disturbingly high proportion of ethnic minority (57 per cent) and white respondents (56 per cent) said they had not discussed their career/higher education plans with a careers advisor prior to starting their current course. Ethnic minority and white students aged 21 and over were less likely to have consulted a careers advisor.

As to why they had decided to take a higher education course, ethnic minority respondents were more likely to say that they had done so due to family pressure or to satisfy family aspirations.

In deciding which higher education institution to study at, a slightly higher proportion of ethnic minority (77 per cent) than white respondents (67 per cent) who were living close to home said distance from home was an important factor. When asked for the one main reason why they had selected their current institution, ethnic minority respondents placed greater emphasis than white respondents on the proximity and reputation of their current institution.

Less than one in five ethnic minority respondents said that a high proportion of ethnic minority students at an institution was an important factor and likely to affect their decision-making.

Chapter 6

Expectation and Reality: Ethnic Minorities in Higher Education

Tony Acland and Waqar Azmi

This chapter examines the expectations and experiences of ethnic minorities in higher education and explores the ways in which universities and colleges can provide a more supportive and encouraging learning environment for these students. The chapter is based upon a case study conducted in one higher education institution[1] and also draws upon research from other educational organisations.

Whilst the debate on race and higher education has tended to centre on issues concerning entry to higher education, especially the controversy over whether there is proper representation, it is also important to consider the nature of ethnic minorities' expectation and experience of higher education. As Leslie Wagner, Vice Chancellor of Leeds Metropolitan University, argued at the recent Leeds conference *Transforming Higher Education:*

> access is not just about admission statistics. The Open University found that 'open door' admissions could be a 'revolving door' as some people entered and quickly left. Access is (also) about when you leave, with what you leave and with what employment opportunities. (Wagner, March 1996)

This chapter shares Leslie Wagner's view that access to higher education (HE) for ethnic minorities extends well beyond entry issues, particularly with reports, such as that by the General,

---

1   We would like to thank all the students and staff, including the Students' Union, clubs and societies of the higher education institution in which the study took place. In particular, we would like to acknowledge Saskia Donald who played a central role both as an organiser and researcher in this project.

Municipal and Boilermakers Union (GMB) (1993) showing that graduates from ethnic minorities are much less likely to find employment than white graduates. Ensuring access to all who have the ability to benefit from higher education requires examining carefully the positive and negative experiences of ethnic minorities throughout their university life. We need to know people's expectations of HE and their actual experiences of academic study and assessment systems, and the appropriateness of support services, counselling, careers guidance, religious provision and student union and club involvement.

To this end, we believe that regular 'action-based research' in a range of universities and colleges is important to enable policy-makers to understand such experiences and to devise ways forward to support and enhance the experiences of students from all ethnic backgrounds. Such a strategy, of course, can only be effective when the research, policy making and implementation are all conducted through partnership between people from different ethnic backgrounds.

As Rose (1991) has argued, detailed case studies are useful for identifying the way different variables interact in complex situations. Obviously, we need a number of such studies in order to identify common issues for ethnic minorities in higher education institutions.

CURRENT PROGRESS

In assessing the ethnic minority experiences and institutional efforts to improve these, it is important to recognise that some progress has been made. Important research aimed at developing practical programmes of action has been conducted. A notable example was the Employment Department funded research in Bristol by John Bird (1992a, 1992b). This research, together with Bird's subsequent publication (Bird, 1996) has been important for stimulating debate on a wide range of access and ethnic experience issues and has led to the development of some effective institutional strategies, such as innovative student mentoring and university–school liaison mechanisms.

Quality audits of universities and colleges testify to the progress which has been made in England. It is pleasing to report, for example, that the Higher Education Quality Council (HEQC) have recently commended the development of equal opportunities measures in many universities:

Of particular note were new appointments policies, access issues, and increased awareness of the need to reflect community demographics in the proportion of ethnic minorities among students and staff. (HEQC, 1996: 88)

However, the HEQC did find some areas for improvement in providing appropriate higher education for ethnic minorities, which we will address later in this paper. In a higher education environment of constant change and tightening of resources, both for institutions and the personal finances of students, this is a matter which requires continual review. Regular monitoring of both ethnic experiences and policy is essential.

IS THERE A COMMON OR DIVERGENT HIGHER EDUCATION EXPERIENCE FOR ETHNIC MINORITIES?

When focusing on ethnic minority experience in higher education, we are confronted with the same dilemmas which researchers face in examining entry statistics to HE, that is, do we concentrate attention on the supposed common ethnic minority experience or give full recognition to the differences between ethnic groups in terms of their distinctive needs? Although we have no wish to sit on the fence on this controversy, we have found that both positions must be addressed. There is certainly a common racist experience reported by some informants from all groups, whilst there are also important differences in the perception of needs and contrasts in the expectations and experiences of, for example, Asian, Muslim and Caribbean students.

This chapter, therefore, focuses on both common and different expectations and experiences of ethnic minorities in higher education. In adopting such an approach we have found it to be also extremely important to pay attention to gender and class differences in expectations and experiences. It should be made clear that we do not consider that gender or class should be treated as independent variables for analysis; rather they are important components in developing an understanding of the complexity of ethnic minorities' experiences.

CASE STUDY: A HIGHER EDUCATION INSTITUTION

Our research examines the nature of ethnic minority expectations of HE life and how such expectations were confirmed or contradicted by their actual experience of studying at a medium-sized higher education institution in the south of England with a staff and student intake which is predominantly white.

The HE institution has a student population of 16,000, over 9,500 of whom are on undergraduate programmes. Approximately 9 per cent of the undergraduate intake identified themselves as of black or ethnic minority origin in 1995. The majority of these students had home addresses from counties outside of the area. Only one ethnic minority student in five came from the local city which had an ethnic minority population of 6 per cent (1991 Census).

Our research is based on a series of focus groups conducted at the institution between 1993 and 1996. A smaller study of Asians in Manchester was conducted in 1994 for comparative purposes. A qualitative research design was chosen in order to uncover how ethnic minorities thought and felt about higher education life. The focus group technique was employed because, as Krueger (1994) has observed, the method is ideal for encouraging small groups to analyse and debate a common issue in a supportive and friendly environment which is not always achievable by conventional one to one interview methods. In fact, we found the method particularly successful in meeting our research goals of looking, not just at the problems, but also at devising institutional strategies to address the situation.

With the help of the Students' Union, the African-Caribbean Society and the Asian Society, ethnic minority students were invited to participate. Separate focus groups were held for Asian and African-Caribbean students.

At the outset, mixed gender groups were used; but females complained of feeling inhibited in front of the males and the majority of focus groups were subsequently conducted in single sex environments, with female groups led by female researchers. Over 150 students participated in the research, with some students contributing to follow-up smaller discussions to explore specific issues.

Although posters inviting people to join discussion groups were prominently placed, most students who attended were those who regularly attended the Asian or African-Caribbean societies. We must accept, therefore, that our study might under-represent the views of ethnic minority students who prefer not to join these groups. As a representative sample is not being claimed, we prefer to refer to focus groups members as 'informants' rather than respondents.

Findings: expectations and reality

Focus group discussions explored a range of issues: reasons for going to higher education; reasons for choosing locations and subjects; expectations of HE; and, in particular, experiences when actually in the institution. Students were asked to give examples of issues which concerned them and which they felt could have inhibited their academic and social performance in the institution. They were also asked what they felt about the way in which the institution responded to their needs and what more could be done to meet their needs and support their successful academic and career progression.

The remainder of this chapter examines some of the key points raised by students in the study and suggests policy revisions and action which higher education institutions should take to improve the learning experiences of ethnic minorities.

Expectations about higher education

Informants were asked: *Why go to HE – is there a special ethnic 'push' factor and is this different for each group?*

Almost all Asian informants, regardless of gender or class, felt that there was a very strong 'push' factor with parents insisting on degree study. Asian parents stressed the importance of education for overcoming racial and socio-economic barriers. One male student summed this up by saying:

> My parents don't want us to have the same struggle as they had. They are determined that I will get a degree and a good job. We know what is expected of us, and we want to be in a good position to look after them in their old age.

Both males and females felt that they had to enter HE for the honour of the family; but those females who had permission to study away from home felt more pressure to succeed because failure would bring too much shame on them and their family. This strong desire to use education to gain or recover a desired high status position confirms other research (such as Acland and Siriwardena, 1989; Ballard and Ballard, 1977) conducted on South Asians in Britain and is important in terms of explaining the greater representation of these groups in higher education.

Some African and Caribbean students spoke in the same way, but most simply stated that parents encouraged them to go to university to get a good career; but made it clear that the choice was very much their own.

Male Asian informants spoke disparagingly about alternatives to higher education available, such as the Youth Training Scheme (YTS). They argued that these should be avoided at all costs, because joining these schemes threatened to lower the status of their family in the community.

With regard to subject choice, all ethnic groups had strong feelings about studying subjects which they and their parents thought to be of high status. In particular, medicine, law and business studies were seen to be appropriate. Of subjects avoided, teacher training was mentioned as a low status, low paid career with plenty of hassle attached to it.

Informants were asked: *Was it important to study at a university near to home or to move away?*

African and Caribbean informants of both sexes expressed few problems with studying away from home, although they preferred to study where there was a thriving ethnic minority community.

Among Asian informants, the place of study was particularly important to females. However, there was some level of consensus that things were changing rapidly. In 1994, some Asian females expressed, with pride, that they were the first in their family to 'break the mould' and had successfully campaigned to study away in order to do the course of their choice. They spoke about others who had too few A-level points to study at a local university and were still not allowed to take up places at institutions which accepted lower points scores in other parts of England.

The overall Asian family push to study what was perceived as high status subjects, such as law or accountancy, increasingly helped to override place of residence as a consideration. However, almost all did not want to study in an institution or a city with few Asians.

Informants were asked: *What do you think of the pre-entry information and visits to the Institute?*

For most African, Caribbean and Asian students, the full-time prospectus was considered to be an important indicator of the suitability of the HE institution for someone of their ethnic background. They looked to the prospectus and other pre-entry information for pictures of Asian or ethnic minority students to see if it was the sort of place where they could fit in. They also hoped for information on facilities and services, such as attention to special dietary or religious provision, as well as evidence of suitable societies or clubs. Students also wanted to know about the ethnic communities near to the institution. They wished to know, for example, whether there were specialist shops and religious centres nearby. Some students expected the prospectuses to go further and stressed the importance of including equal opportunity statements, supported by details of how this would be backed up in practice.

Surprisingly, pre-visits seemed to have little impact on perceptions, with opinions varying considerably on the nature of the institution and the city.

Reality: the experience of higher education

When we asked informants about their actual experience of academic and social life in the institution, we found that reality differed somewhat from expectations.

Some African, Caribbean and Asian informants expected the curriculum to reflect a growing multi-cultural campus. In this respect, the reality of the curriculum which they actually encountered disappointed them. They recognised that social science and media studies had specialist optional race or ethnic minority studies units; but they were concerned that there were too few of these and, more important, the mainstream core units on most courses overlooked ethnic minority studies and equal opportunity issues.

There is independent evidence to suggest that this is a common situation in English universities and colleges. The HEQC noted in their 'Learning from the Second Audit' report: 'of all the areas of policy, equal opportunities has made least impact on the curriculum' (HEQC, 1996: 28).

Students who were on courses which required work placements were very concerned, particularly as it was common practice to supply photographs to agencies taking students. Because they felt that it was a naive practice which allowed employers to discriminate, some students had asked tutors to stop sending photographs to prospective agencies. Some students also felt that better paid placements tended to go to white students, with ethnic minority students more likely to get unpaid or less useful in-house placements. Although an investigation by the institution's equal opportunities committee failed to find objective evidence to substantiate this latter perception, it was considered important for faculties to review their work placement procedures to ensure that they were manifestly fair to all and provided no opportunity for racial discrimination by external agencies.

Many students, especially those in the first year of study, 1994, were disappointed at the relatively few numbers of students from ethnic minority backgrounds, particularly on some courses. This was compounded by their disquiet, even alarm, at the very small numbers of ethnic minority teaching staff. Such a situation made it difficult for students to adjust to life away from home and to cope with the impersonality of studying in such a large institution.

For many students, Students' Union societies, particularly the Asian and African-Caribbean societies, helped them enormously to find friends, develop support groups and share experiences. They found these self-support groups to be much more successful in addressing ethnic minority needs than the formal mechanisms of support provided by the Institution.

All focus groups were asked: *Have you experienced racism since entering higher education?*

The prevalence of racism stimulated debate and disagreement. Whilst some students reported little or no experience of racism at college, others reported a number of incidents.

Few thought the Institute to be worse than that experienced at previous colleges. Nevertheless, there were reports from all groups noting racist comments and attitudes by other students. Some students felt that they had experienced discrimination in classes and assessment by a small minority of staff.

Informants pointed out that some incidents might appear to others to be trivial, but, when combined with the totality of ethnic minority experience at university, make them feel both different and unwanted. Examples of such incidents included: staff making insensitive comments about ethnic minority people; lecturers using inappropriate 'ethnic minority' metaphors; and tutors simply making no effort to use the students' first names (even relatively easy names of Caribbean female students). When asked, 'What should be done about this?' students saw it as a staff development issue. As one male Caribbean student commented:

Staff need training on how to treat ethnic minority students.

A minority of Asian, African and Caribbean students, particularly males, alleged that some staff might have discriminated against them in marking assignments or examination papers. When asked if the anonymous marking pilot scheme should be extended to all courses in the institution, almost all agreed that this would promote confidence in the fairness and impartiality of the assessment process.

It should be noted that student led organisations were not immune from racist allegations. For example, Students' Union sports clubs were accused by Caribbean males of being racist. A clique of white male friends were said to dominate certain sports clubs and they selected their friends regardless of ability.

Focus groups were asked to consider if there was sufficient institute support regarding specialist advice and guidance on race issues. Almost all students felt that there was a need for a specialist race officer, or, if this was not possible, an equal opportunities officer. All felt that this person should be from the ethnic minority community who had experienced racism and the problems of studying in a predominantly white institution. Informants complained about the lack of such provision and tended to use unofficial authority figures from the ethnic minority community, usually a sympathetic ethnic minority or Asian lecturer.

This brings us to what the informants believed to be a central problem with the institution, which was the perceived absence of sufficient ethnic minority role models. Virtually all students complained about the lack of ethnic minority lecturers in the institution, and for females, the over-representation of males. This was seen as crucial for a number of reasons. First, it made them suspicious about the organisation's commitment to equal opportunities. Second, they wondered how a predominantly white male staff could empathise with their needs and freely communicate with them. Third, as noted previously, many were desperate to consult and discuss racist experiences with someone who would understand at first hand. However, most of all, they were concerned with the lack of successful role models, which most considered vital for building the confidence that they, too, could 'make it'.

When informants were asked about the appropriateness of the institution's specialist facilities and services, considerable differences in opinions were expressed between students from different ethnic backgrounds. Comments reflected their specific cultural needs. For example, some Caribbean females wanted specialist hairdressing facilities on campus.

The strongest views on specialist facilities were expressed by Muslim males who were concerned with the provision of prayer rooms for males and females, with appropriate washing facilities. The institution's policy of permitting ordinary classrooms to be booked when available was considered to be inadequate. With increased numbers of Muslims in the institute, including overseas students, demands for such facilities increased during the period of the study. However, in responding to such special resource needs, institutional managers pointed out that the newer HE organisations received substantially less funding per student compared to 'old' universities. Managers argued that this made it difficult to find resources for special interest groups. It is a sad irony that it is the newer sectors of HE where minorities enter most frequently that have less resources to attend to specific needs.

CONCLUSION

Following the growing number of institutional studies, many universities and colleges have introduced programmes to improve the experience of ethnic minority students. Improvements to access and admission systems and student support services were recognised in a recent national Higher Education Quality Council report (HEQC, 1996). However, it would be wrong to be complacent and to exaggerate the achievements in addressing these issues. Much more needs to be done to eradicate the possibility of racism and to develop new strategies for improving the experience of ethnic minorities in higher education.

Institutions need to grasp the nettle and provide special resources to support minority groups. Practical measures are needed of the kind which Bird has recommended (1992b, 1996), with responsibility for implementing change shared by central services, administration and each academic department. However, following our research, we would like to particularly recommend the following measures which should be given serious consideration by educational policy-makers:

- Prospectuses and other pre-entry information should contain pictures and accurate information on ethnic minority students, communities, special facilities and equal opportunities policies and procedures.
- Regular monitoring should be conducted to compare ethnic minority groups for admissions, progression, retention, achievement and first destination (employment) rates compared to white students. Statistical analysis is insufficient and should be enriched by surveys to ascertain minority groups' learning experiences.
- Curricula, particularly core units, should include equal opportunity and ethnic minority issues where possible.

- Anonymous marking of assignments and examination scripts should become universal practice to increase confidence in the assessment process.
- If work placements are required on courses, care should be taken to prevent potential for discrimination by agencies, eg no photographs should be issued.
- Applications for academic and senior management posts from minority groups should be encouraged, eg by advertising in ethnic minority newspapers.
- Teaching and front line service staff must receive training in sensitive and appropriate communication with ethnic minorities.
- More facilities for ethnic minorities are needed. Not only should the Institution provide facilities, such as prayer rooms, but the Students' Union should also take responsibility by encouraging ethnic clubs and societies and ensuring equal representation in sports and leisure activities.
- A 'One Stop' facility should be available so that ethnic minority students can obtain direct help and support with problems or issues which arise. This may be achieved in alternative ways by different institutions, with some providing a specialist race officer and others an equal opportunities or student affairs manager.
- More liaison with local schools and colleges is needed, including attention to mentoring for different age groups. Such access measures should include Compact Arrangements which recognise the needs of, for example, local Asian females who wish to study at their local university.

In a period of reduced funding for higher education, some higher education institutions may be reluctant to allocate funds for the specialist needs of ethnic minority students. Particularly controversial issues, such as the provision of Muslim prayer rooms in a secular institution, may be easily lost in a resource-conscious university. However, there is one economic argument which might persuade institutions to make efforts to improve services and facilities for ethnic minorities. A number of universities compete to increase their overseas student admissions, with markets particularly buoyant in countries with Muslim populations. Provision of such facilities, accurately advertised, could result in increased overseas admissions.

For those institutions who are committed to equal opportunities, an important question is 'who within the university should be responsibility for devising effective strategies to improve the experience of ethnic minorities?' The view taken here is consistent with that advocated in the recent *Higher Education and Equality: A Guide* (1997) issued jointly by the Commission for Racial Equality, the Equal Opportunities Commission and the Committee of Vice Chancellors and Principals. According to this view, radical institutional changes designed to improve equal opportunities must be driven from the top, by governing bodies, academic boards and vice chancellors. Under enthusiastic leadership, it should be the responsibility of all managers and course leaders to implement centrally generated equal opportunities policies, particularly ensuring that both formal and informal systems function to adequately support all student groups.

If major changes are to be made, the leadership must ultimately come from central government and the Department for Education and Employment (DfEE). In particular, the agencies which monitor the quality of provision, particularly HEQC and HEFCE (now the QAA), could use their powers to ensure that institutions provide suitable facilities and services. For example, HEFCE could insist that subject assessments include a grading for 'suitability of curricula for ethnic minority students'. Similarly, HEQC could increase priority given to institutional specialist provision for such students, including campus facilities for special religious needs where more than 50 students request it. It is pleasing to note that these agencies have started to implement some measures during 1997, such as the provision of rigorous equal opportunity guidelines for subject assessors. This indicates that they are prepared to take an important lead in this matter and it will be interesting to see whether this results in real improvements in institutional support for ethnic minority students.

Chapter 7

Towards a Black Construct
of Accessibility

Paul Michael Allen

THE RESEARCH CONTEXT

The research that follows represents a small part of a longitudinal study of black students studying on three higher education courses at a former polytechnic, now a new university in the West Midlands. The study sought to highlight the perceptions and experiences of black students in higher education.[1] A previous study at the same institution had found that although most black students were satisfied with their course, a minority had criticised the lack of a 'race' element within such programmes. The study had concluded that:

> This contradiction between overall satisfaction and the acknowledged ethnocentric nature of the higher education curriculum is worth pursuing at greater length than this short project allows. (Housee et al, 1990)

My qualitative research conducted between 1989 and 1993 was an attempt to build on and update previous findings through semi-structured in-depth taped interviews of 50 black students. Indeed, some of my findings endorsed certain aspects of previous research; however, my study sought to explore more fully the existence of black identities in higher education. For the purpose of this chapter I have highlighted some of the key issues that emanated from the research. These included: the curriculum, black informal networks, staffing, employment destinations, and a black construct of

---

1   The term 'black' will be used to refer to people of African, African-Caribbean and Asian origin.

accessibility. I will go on to argue that a black perspective does exist in higher education (Brienburg, 1987), and that such a perspective is linked to a critical cultural stand-point that I have called 'black scepticality'.

RACISM, REPRESENTATION AND THE CURRICULUM

The central theme that came out of the questioning of black students in my study was the extent to which racism was perceived to be part and parcel of the higher education terrain, as these three comments from one male and two females illustrate:

> When I lived with white students, the first time I came into the kitchen they all went silent. Later on they told me they thought I had come to rob the place.

> The accommodation person for the Halls of Residence didn't want to give me a flat. But she offered it to white students. I realised the person was racist, she could defend her actions. It would be your word against hers.

> I notice sometimes with Asian students when they are being talked to by the lecturers they actually explain something to them slowly as though they have not got the sense to understand what's being said. If they have got to read something out they will be asked if they can manage it. To get on this course you have to have sense, but they don't seem to take that into consideration.

The last comment in particular suggests that racism does not necessarily manifest itself in the overt 'Alf Garnett' manner. Much of the time racism is subtle; it is the glance, and the unsaid. It is these kinds of experiences that many black students often have to endure on their passage through higher education and beyond. Rosen (1990), in her research on black and white students at North London Polytechnic (now University of North London), argued that 'the black experience was mainly ignored or given token acknowledgement' (p.93).

Debates about curriculum control and eurocentricity have in the past mainly focused on secondary education and the structuring of knowledge. It is only in recent times that higher education has come under close scrutiny concerning its multicultural or anti-racist subject provision, a point highlighted by Williams et al, who asked:

> Why has the higher education curriculum been subject to so little scrutiny? Courses in humanities and social sciences, for example, ostensibly value personal experiences, but frequently fail to recognise

and validate knowledge, culture and experience from black communities. Other subject areas may not even make rhetorical claims of
interest or question their ethnocentrcity. (Williams et al, 1989: 25)

My research indicated that many black students were unhappy with
aspects of the curriculum. One second year student commented that:

> I think certain modules didn't give any consideration to racial equality
> issues, especially the ones I've done, like Social Policy. I can't say they
> have given any consideration to it.

Two second year female students stated:

> I cannot relate to high art, it's just not me. I tend to explore issues con-
> cerned with black people. I feel English heritage doesn't belong to me.

> I think race issues need to be a compulsory part of all module choices
> available to students, and not just an option. In this way it can be dealt
> with at all levels within the polytechnic and not shunned as a radical
> arena for debate.

These comments reflected strongly the overall dissatisfaction in the
way that anti-racism had failed to permeate their courses in a more
rigorous way. Other black students felt that some of the white
lecturers found it difficult to relate to black students as these two
comments from final year students suggested:

> I did feel that issues of race were not tackled properly, it was skimmed.
> I think it is the way lecturers are, there is not a lot of understanding. I
> don't know, its hard, you can't make them understand the way you feel
> as a person and your experience.

> Lecturers don't want to talk about it (race). They are racist themselves.
> Those who do are patronising to black students. In essays they don't
> want to know about your experiences, only what white researchers have
> found.

The second comment in particular, raises issues about aspects of the
learning process which may allow the subtleties of racism to operate.
The assessment system and the hidden nature of the evaluation
process on many courses may sometimes enhance prevalent
stereotypes regarding the ability of black students to achieve.
Indeed, evidence cited by Crace (1995), at the University of East
London, carried out a test where black and white students submitted
each other's work under each other's registration numbers, often as
well known to teaching staff as the students themselves. This
experiment did appear to show that black students were marked
down.

In my own study black students questioned the relevance of the curriculum when it failed to introduce their specific experiences of being black into the classroom and lecture hall. In many ways the black students in the study were driven to find an alternative curriculum, that is one that acknowledged such black heroes as Dubois, King, Malcolm X, Gandhi, CLR James, Marcus Garvey, Black Panthers, H. Tubman etc. Students actively found black bookshops and used such material to counter what they saw as a form of eurocentric bias. It is clear that many black students are rigorously questioning the whole basis of what they are being taught in terms of 'objective academia'; more and more the issue of relevance is becoming central to their personal and group constructs of their identities.

BLACK INFORMAL NETWORKS:
THE CREATION OF 'BLACK SPACE'

Resistance lies in self-conscious engagement with dominant, normative discourses and representations and in the active creation of oppositional analytical and cultural spaces. Uncovering and reclaiming subjugated knowledge is one way to lay claim to alternative histories. (Mohanty, 1994: 148)

One of the key findings that came out of my own interviews with black students was they way in which they formed their own informal support mechanisms within the higher education institution. Particular black meeting places were identified within the institution, the most important of which was located on a group of tables in the canteen where predominantly between 20 and 50 African-Caribbean and Asian students would congregate, and discuss the pedagogies and practices of the institution. It was in the realm of this 'black space' where black realities, identities and strategies were continually being replenished by the informal group. Many black students actively developed a proactive educational and cultural network as the following comments illustrate:

People will help you with books etc. In the first year we worked as a team. This brings you into contact with other blacks and from that a relationship is formed.

It was noticeable that this black support network operated both inside and outside the classroom and there was a tendency for other black students to move towards the group, as a male student observed:

> Although we sat together collectively in groups (in lectures) we didn't
> know each other... it was an unconscious thing.

The black informal network had been observed and commented upon
by white students as one black female student recalled:

> They (white students) ask you why you black students go around in
> groups.

Through distorted representations, the black informal network may
be perceived by white students and others in a more pathological
light. It became evident that the black informal network had a variety
of educational and political functions, it was the arena where black
students had their own space to devise strategies and work through
problems encountered within the institution and to talk generally,
as embellished by this female student who stated:

> It (the informal group) gives you a sense of security, it motivates you to
> discuss things and deal with it. It gives you mutual support and
> counselling. The moral support means that you have got to get through
> for yourselves and for black people generally. We are in a white
> institution, we have to encourage each other to be proud. We are role
> models.

The informal discussions that took place in the 'social spaces' of the
institution were crucial on a deeper level for these particular black
students, because they felt extra pressure in terms of succeeding as
black people. Edwards (1990), in her study of black and white women
in higher education, found that the black women felt under great
scrutiny because of their race. Hence they felt a responsibility to
others of their race to achieve. In some ways this is not surprising in
that black people have been historically constructed and stereotyped
as a 'problematic group' (Carby, 1982; Solomos, 1989). Indeed, the
creation of the black informal network at another level perhaps tells
us a great deal about the ethos and culture of higher education
institutions.

My research across the institution indicated that on other courses
some black students felt very isolated, as the following two
comments suggest:

> The more I was looking around the more I was the only black person
> there... I do feel as if I am on my own because if you have got somebody
> who is really, say, black and they are with you on the course then you do
> tend to feel more secure don't you?

We used to sit in with the degree students on Thurdays, there was only one black person on the degree. Both groups sat separately... Other students don't want to mix with us because we are all black. Other than our own group, nobody wants to talk to us.'

Without doubt the development of the informal black network is an increasingly important phenomenon, but just as important is the need for educational institutions to put in place more formalised structures where black students can deal with problems that may occur on courses and on placements.

THE LANGUAGE AND LOGIC OF BLACK SCEPTICALITY

The shared perceptions of their position within the institution and a conscious affirmation of their 'blackness' led the students in my study to viewing the particular practices of the institution from a critical cultural location. This stance is what I have called 'black scepticality', which operates as a specialised body of thought, that is mobilised by black students moving through contemporary white higher educational structures. Black scepticality operates through a variety of different levels; it is related to personal experience of specific interactions, biography, group identification and institutional ethos. At the heart of black scepticality are focal concerns, like: where does my history and culture fit into what I am learning; why is it not validated within the institutional ethos, culture and curriculum; who is around to support me and validate my right to question what I am being taught and my right to be here?

Black scepticality interrogates the legitimacy of institutional knowledge claims in the light of one's own lived reality. It can be viewed as the partial unmasking of eurocentric and racist ideologies, subtle and unsubtle, ingrained in higher educational structures. It is, therefore, in the corridor, in the lecture hall, in the canteen and in the mind where black scepticality is kept alive. Black scepticality operates at different positions on a continuum and in different contexts. For some black students scepticality operates at group level and is a major factor that structures their lived experience, for others it may be more submerged or subliminal. For example, one female student in the author's study had said that she did not see herself as someone who defended black issues. However, in her discussions she pointed to failures in her course to deliver important elements of multiculturalism: 'you don't do anything that comes under Afro-Caribbeans full stop'.

Black sceptically becomes a conscious or even unconscious way of locating oneself and others within the overarching culture of the institution. Banton (1988) has pointed to the complex levels of what he calls 'racial consciousness', which has relevance to black scepticality. Thus Banton argues that:

> In one form it (racial consciousness) is an individual's interpretation of how his or her life is affected by the ways others assign him or her to a racial category. In another form, it is an individual's tendency to assign others to 'racial' categories. While racial consciousness varies from one person to another, there are also common elements. If those who are assigned to a particular category are treated similarly they are likely to share this experience. (Banton, 1988: 9)

The evidence presented in this section appears to point to the existence of a black scepticality which shapes black students outlook within the institution.

STAFFING THE 'IVORY TOWER'

It was clear from student comments that many of them felt that more black teaching staff were required on their courses and within the institution as a whole. For these students, the perceived lack of black staff spoke volumes about the institutions's real commitment to racial equality. Research has continually shown the importance of having black role models in professional and academic positions (Swann, 1985; Siraj-Blatchford, 1990; Moyo-Robbins, 1995). The following comments from two third-year female students were indicative of this concern, particularly in the teaching of race options:

> I tend to be dubious of white lecturers because they are not black. I tend to be sceptical. How can they know? They are not black. If a black person was teaching me I would feel differently.

> We need more black staff as role models. It is not nice to be surrounded by only white people.

The research of Housee et al (1990) and Bird et al (1991) adds further weight to the author's findings on this issue and presents substantial testimonies from black students regarding a deep seated concern over the apparent lack of black staff within their respective institutions. The black lecturer, who is often isolated within white educational institutions, has to juggle the demands of a racist educational structure with the need to maintain credibility with black students.

Like other professions in Britain, the academic establishment has been slow to respond to the multiracial nature of British society and has continued to argue that its 'meritocratic' selection procedures are clear and fair. However, this ignores the reality of hidden cultural and institutional barriers that work to the detriment of black applicants (Sargeant and Walker, 1992; Singh, Chapter 11 of this book). As with the admissions process to higher education, the balance of power in the labour-market recruitment process lies deeply embedded in institutional contexts of the bureaucracy. In this situation there is a tendency for white organisations, consciously or unconsciously, to bias the rules in favour of white majority applications (Jenkins, 1986).

DEGREES AND DESTINATIONS

The foreboding that was expressed by the majority of students in terms of their career prospects has been supported by empirical research on labour-market destinations (Ballard and Holden, 1975; Brennan and McGeevor, 1990). Cumulatively, such research has shown that black graduates make more applications than their white counterparts and yet gain fewer interviews. They are less likely to find themselves in the job they initially would have preferred, and more likely to feel overqualified for the job they had. The type of course taken by black students, in comparison to white students, largely determined their employment prospects. In summation of these findings Singh (1990) has commented that such experiences must influence black students' views of the value of higher education as well as their motivation and career aspirations.

TOWARDS A BLACK CONSTRUCT OF ACCESSIBILITY

A black model of accessibility is concerned with black student and staff recruitment, through the higher education sector as a whole, particularly in areas where there is severe black under-representation. There is a need for a more responsive and relevant injection of black culture into the curriculum. There is a requirement for positive support and guidance for black students as they pass through the institution, along with consciousness raising sessions with black staff either formally or informally. This construct acknowledges the way racial discrimination operates in the labour-market and seeks, through adequate on-going careers advice and workshops sessions, to equip students with the skills to confront positively situations where they are disadvantaged because of their colour. Direct institutional intervention can be made by a higher education provider by scrutinising the recruitment policies in terms of race of prospective employers who attend various 'milk rounds' and can thus feed such information back to the black student population so students can make informed judgements about possible employers.

A number of developments are needed to combat the barriers experienced by black students:

1. The appointment of black liaison officers at senior levels in higher education is an important requirement for monitoring racial discrimination and harassment.
2. The development of formalised black student support networks to liaise with and advise the academic boards of higher education institutions.
3. The inclusion in all higher education institutions of core race modules, particularly for white students.
4. The development of a rolling programme of anti-racist staff development sessions for all staff.
5. Institutions of higher education must be prepared to get involved with their localised black communities by fostering long-term outreach provision.

Those proposals mentioned are not a panacea for achieving racial equality in higher education, rather they represent an incremental move towards that goal. At a time when equal opportunities and positive action policies are being dismantled by those on the right, and the left is in a state of identity crisis, the issue of creating wider educational access to higher education for black students appears more rhetorical than real.

In the light of the evidence presented in this chapter, one has to consider deeply what 'access' really means for black students. A black construct of access has to concern itself not just with institutional entry but with progression, cultural representation and labour-market destinations. The evidence indicates that, in terms of achieving racial equality, institutions of higher education still have a long way to go and increasingly black students are questioning institutional commitment, whilst experiencing institutional indifference.

A higher education system which is relevant to the needs of black people must truly acknowledge the barriers that exist in a white society and give due respect to the struggles and strategies that black learners have to develop in order to survive. For the crucial question that a black student population poses at this time is not simply an issue of equal access to existing educational power structures, but of ultimately finding ways of transforming them so they become blacker in culture, blacker in ethos and blacker in understanding; the ivory tower must come down!

Chapter 8

Race, Culture and the Curriculum

Alicear Jiwani and Terry Regan

What makes the University of East London such an interesting place to study in at present is that it is where cultural geographies of the Old and New East End meet on ground of neither's making. (Cohen, 1995)

INTRODUCTION

Research into ethnic minority participation in higher education is becoming an area of study warranting attention as the number of ethnic minority students continues to grow. The participation rate for ethnic minority students is far greater than for those of the indigenous population. Previous research tended to concentrate on access to higher education for individuals from the various ethnic minority communities. More recent research has attempted to take the subject further by looking at the experience and performance of ethnic minority students.

Singh (1990), for example, reported the results of a survey of 858 students attending the Bradford and Ilkley Community College on the Diploma of Higher Education course from 1975 to 1982. Although the sample of ethnic minority students from that survey was relatively small (14 per cent), the findings (that ethnic minority students were more likely to be non-standard entrants, and had higher drop-out rates than white students) are nevertheless important. The research also pointed to a number of findings relating to the experience of ethnic minority students.

Researchers are increasingly pointing to the need to look beyond access and participation rates and at the experiences of students from ethnic minority communities in higher education institutions (for example, Arora, 1995, and several authors in this book). Areas of particular concern include whether the process of assessment experienced by ethnic minority students is fair and non-discriminatory, whether the institution monitors the progress and performance of ethnic minority students and whether curriculum content recognises and provides for issues of culture and race.

Another area of concern is the lack of ethnic minority staff, which, it is argued, is having a profound impact on the experiences of ethnic minority students.

> The CRE informed the Education, Science and Arts Committee of the House of Commons in January (CRE, 1989) that there is unlikely to be any increase in the supply of black teachers in the 1990s. The CRE suggested that the racism and racial discrimination experienced by black students at all levels within and outside the education system was to blame. (Siraj-Blatchford, 1990)

This is a topic discussed further by Gurhurpal Singh in Chapter 11 of this book.

Twitchin (1995) claims in his paper, *Staff Development in Multi-cultural Practice,* that how higher education institutions manage the 'learning experience for ethnic minority and overseas students has become a key issue'. He argues that within the trend of 'increasing cultural diversity among students and staff and in the world for which students are being prepared' in-service training for staff is a priority. The research findings from our study suggest that the ability of higher education institutions, especially the new universities, to reflect issues of race and culture, nationality and religion in curriculum content are likely to become key issues.

Against the background of a high participation rate for ethnic minority students in higher education institutions, particularly in the new universities (Modood, 1993), how students of ethnic minority backgrounds fare needs to be investigated. Their expectations, experiences and the content of the curriculum on offer to them have been raised in some of the current literature (McCarthy, 1990; Singh, 1990; Siraj-Blatchford, 1990). These areas should now be considered to warrant as much, if not more, attention as that given to access.

The question of whether race, culture, nationality and religion should be reflected in curriculum content was not surveyed in isolation. The study undertaken at the University of East London covered the areas of equal opportunities policy, ethnic monitoring procedures, staff recruitment and development, staff training in race and ethnic relations, curriculum development, research, methods of teaching and student assessment, staff and student grievance procedures, student welfare, tutorial and pastoral support, student representation, university initiatives in the community, proposals for new structures, procedures and projects and majority/minority relations.

The commissioning of the study at the University of East London (UEL) stems from a background of discussions which have been ongoing for some time. The institution is also in the process of developing a strategy for implementation of its equal opportunities policy and according to the invitation to tender document:

> The University is appointing a Commission of Enquiry to Review Policies and Practices on Race and Ethnicity during the academic year 1995–96. This research is intended to provide some essential background data to inform the Commission of Enquiry and assist in the formulation of future policy.

This chapter puts forward the views of both staff and students on whether race, culture, religion and nationality should be reflected in curriculum content, the possible ways in which this can be achieved and the benefits of doing so. Finally, it looks at the issue of reflecting race and culture in the curriculum from the wider perspective of whether higher education is about educating and preparing individuals for the outside world and about personal growth, whatever or however that is defined. Again, this is achieved by presenting the views of respondents.

Both quantitative and qualitative approaches were taken to the collection and analysis of data. The staff questionnaire was mailed to 150 members of staff. The student survey was carried out among students by subject area. The collection of qualitative data followed on from the analysis of quantitative data from the questionnaire surveys. Data from staff were obtained by interview of respondents from the questionnaire survey, with individuals selected in the various job categories. Staff were also given the opportunity to be interviewed, if they wished, to discuss any area of concern raised by the survey, irrespective of their job status. Qualitative data from students were obtained by means of focus group discussions and debate of the areas outlined above.

SUMMARY PROFILE OF STUDENTS AND STAFF IN THE SURVEY

The profile of those students surveyed shows that the majority were under 25, with the largest group being in the 21–24 years old age category. Aggregation of the figures shows that of those responding,

77 per cent were mature students. The gender breakdown of those sampled produced a majority (58.6 per cent) of female respondents. This is a direct result of some of the courses/subject areas surveyed, which appear to be predominantly female orientated.

The marital status of the majority (64.2 per cent) of respondents was single. However, just over 30 per cent were either married or living with a partner. Almost one in four (24 per cent) of respondents reported having dependants. On the matter of disability, the questionnaire shows 2.4 per cent of students reporting themselves as disabled, as compared to 2.6 per cent in the University's recently completed student feedback questionnaire.

The largest group of students gained entry with the traditional A-level qualifications (44.2 per cent), with less than 1 per cent gaining entry with no qualifications at all. Over one in ten respondents fell in each of the Access (14.3 per cent), BTEC National (11.1 per cent) and Other (13.3 per cent) categories. The educational establishment previously attended by the majority of respondents was college (66.8 per cent), and this figure would include those whose qualifications for entry were Access, as well as some A-level entrants and others with lower qualifications.

English was the mother tongue language for 65 per cent of the sample. An analysis by ethnic origin found that large proportions of Bangladeshi (93.9 per cent), Chinese (89.5 per cent), Indian (92.6 per cent), Malaysian (88.9 per cent), Pakistani (83.3 per cent) and Other Asian (95.5 per cent) students did not have English as their mother tongue language. However, only 9.7 per cent claimed to have a problem with either speaking, reading or writing English.

Responses were obtained from every category of staff sampled. These were Deans and above, heads of department, subject co-ordinators, non-teaching management and departmental secretaries. One of the reasons for limiting the survey to senior staff members was to ensure that the study captured the views and perceptions of those individuals who are likely to be policy-makers, and whose thinking on these issues is likely to be translated into action.

SHOULD RACE, CULTURE, NATIONALITY AND RELIGION BE REFLECTED IN CURRICULUM CONTENT?

The results of the staff survey show that almost half of those responding to the question of whether culture, religion, race and nationality should be reflected in curriculum content, thought that it should (Table 8.1). 48 per cent of respondents thought that the curriculum content should reflect these issues, and that this would be of benefit to both students and staff (Table 8.2).

Table 8.1　　**Should race, culture, nationality and religion be reflected in curriculum content? (staff sample)**

Response	Number	%
Yes	22	48
No	13	28
Don't know	5	11
No answer	6	13

Although the sample is relatively small, it represents a response rate of one in three. A degree of significance, therefore, may be attributed to the number who said 'yes', as it indicates that policy-makers may be favourably disposed to the whole question of whether race, culture etc should be reflected in curriculum content.

The proportion of staff respondents agreeing that race, culture, religion and nationality should be reflected in the curriculum was less than a half, compared with a majority (60.9 per cent) who thought that these issues should be reflected in the style/method of teaching. The number of respondents agreeing that race, culture etc should be reflected in curriculum content was also less than the number who believed that incorporation of these issues would be beneficial, as Table 8.2 illustrates.

Table 8.2　　**Groups that would benefit by having race/cultural issues reflected in the curriculum (staff sample)**

Response	Number	%
All students	23	50
Some students	2	4
Staff	10	22
No answer	21	46

The results of the student survey revealed that, whilst a majority of the sample was against the inclusion of these issues, over four in ten students (41.7 per cent) believed that they should be accounted for in the curriculum (Table 8.3). There is thus a critical mass of students who believe their inclusion to be of importance.

Table 8.3   Should race, culture, nationality and religion be reflected in curriculum content? (student sample)

Response	Number	%
Yes	361	42
No	504	58

Missing cases = 72

Disaggregation of the student results by ethnicity shows that three ethnic groups had majorities believing that culture, religion, race and nationality should be reflected in curriculum content (Table 8.4). Most prominent among them were the small 'mixed parentage' category, with 61.1 per cent of respondents agreeing with this. Overall the 'White English' group is no less in agreement than students as a whole (42.1 per cent against 41.7 per cent) with this proposition, although a majority of respondents in this category nevertheless do still disagree with their inclusion. Interestingly, the 'Black African' group exactly reflects the overall proportion of 'White English' respondents in agreement.

Examination of the data by age shows only the 35–39 age group with a majority of respondents believing that culture, race, religion and nationality should be included in curriculum content, with all of the other groups showing 'no' outweighing 'yes' respondents. Those least in favour are quite clearly those under the age of 21, where over two in three (67.6 per cent) are against this notion.

Analysis by gender reveals male respondents much less likely to favour inclusion of these issues into curriculum content than their female counterparts. Nevertheless majorities of both groups do not favour their inclusion, although for women the result is fairly evenly balanced.

The percentage of student respondents in favour of reflecting race, culture, nationality and religion in curriculum content was slightly lower than the figure obtained for respondents' perception of the importance of ethnic minority staff. Large majorities of all ethnic groups thought that it was 'very' or 'quite' important to have ethnic minority staff. In terms of those who thought it was 'unimportant', both the 'White English' (37.3 per cent) and the 'White Other' (32.9 per cent) groups were more likely to think in this way than were respondents as a whole (25.7 per cent).

Table 8.4 **Disaggregation of student results by ethnicity**

	Yes		No		All	
	Number	%	Number	%	Number	%
Ethnic origin						
Bangladeshi	9	29	22	71	31	100
Black African	45	42	62	58	107	100
Black Caribbean	31	58	22	42	53	100
Black Other	13	59	9	41	22	100
Chinese	5	29	12	71	17	100
Indian	20	38	33	62	53	100
Irish	10	43	13	57	23	100
Jewish	6	46	7	54	13	100
Malaysian	8	29	20	71	28	100
Mixed parentage	11	61	7	39	18	100
Pakistani	11	50	11	50	22	100
Other Asian	3	25	9	75	12	100
White English	159	43	211	57	370	100
White Other	21	33	43	67	64	100
Other	6	46	7	54	13	100

Respondents were asked whether being taught by an ethnic or other minority member of staff would be beneficial in any or all of four areas in their studies (Table 8.5). The results revealed that being taught by an ethnic minority member of staff was felt by almost a quarter of the total sample (24.1 per cent) to be beneficial to the course being studied. While having ethnic minority staff would suit the learning style of 16.9 per cent, they would be beneficial to only just over 11 per cent in the way they were assessed. By far the largest number of responses (46.4 per cent) were obtained from students who thought that ethnic minority staff would be beneficial to their overall learning experience.

There was little obvious, consistent trend by age in response to these questions, perhaps most notable being the high percentages of those in the 25–29 age bracket agreeing to each, when compared to their peers. Indeed in this age group some 55.2 per cent thought that being taught by a member of staff from an ethnic minority would benefit their overall learning experience.

Analysed by gender, the greatest observable difference occurs in terms of ethnic minority staff being beneficial to the overall learning experience of students, with 52.3 per cent of female compared to 38.1 per cent of male respondents believing this to be the case. Male respondents were more likely to agree to the beneficial aspect of such staff on their style of learning and to the way they were assessed.

Table 8.5   Benefits from being taught by an ethnic minority member of staff (student sample)

	Course studied		Style of learning		Way assessed		Overall learning	
	Number	%	Number	%	Number	%	Number	%
Ethnic origin								
Bangladeshi	6	18	6	18	4	12	13	39
Black African	33	28	36	31	30	25	53	45
Black Caribbean	16	29	9	16	17	31	30	55
Black Other	7	25	6	21	7	25	16	57
Chinese	5	26	5	26	8	42	9	47
Indian	12	22	16	29	10	18	24	44
Irish	5	21	1	4	0	–	20	83
Jewish	3	21	0	–	1	7	6	43
Malaysian	6	21	9	32	7	25	10	36
Mixed parentage	8	40	4	20	3	15	15	75
Pakistani	6	25	4	17	2	8	10	42
Other Asian	8	36	4	18	0		8	36
White English	87	22	42	11	9	2	171	43
White Other	17	24	12	17	5	7	37	52
Other	3	20	2	13	2	13	4	27

REFLECTING RACE, CULTURE, NATIONALITY AND RELIGION IN CURRICULUM CONTENT

The remainder of this chapter sets out the responses obtained from staff and students on how the issue of reflecting race, culture, religion and nationality in the curriculum might be achieved. All of the comments received have been placed into six broad categories, and individuals may have comments placed in one or more, depending upon the number of points which they made. Whilst these categories are necessarily subjective, it is believed that they have sufficient coherence to help explain the diverse points made by respondents. In Tables 8.6 – 8.11 the percentage figures are based on the number in each ethnic group who actually made comments in the relevant category.

The first category of response concerns the sizeable number of comments which suggested that culture, religion, race and nationality should be included where relevant. Some individuals provided little clue as to whether they thought they should be included on their own specific course. Some thought that there were areas in which these issues applied, and these were invariably in the social sciences. A Black Caribbean respondent thought that it depended 'on the course you are undertaking eg Sociology or Cultural Studies [or] Psychology'. Other students also expressed some noteworthy concerns, among them that inclusion should be demand-led, and should not unduly increase the amount of time required for studying:

> If the demand exists, but not just to be progressive or PC.

> It really depends on the courses done – there is limited time to fit it into all courses.

Table 8.6 reveals the percentage of the listed groups citing 'where relevant', and shows a much higher percentage of both 'Black Caribbean' and 'White' respondents represented here.

Table 8.6   Students who thought race/cultural issues should be included 'where relevant'

cell percentages

Ethnic origin	%
Black African	7
Black Caribbean	29
Indian	5
White	27
All others	8

Another category of respondents thought that the issues were already included on their course. Table 8.7 shows that this is not a very widespread strand of thought, and indeed this view appears almost entirely restricted to those individuals on courses where ethnicity, culture and race are integral to the learning and under-standing of the subject.

Table 8.7   Students who thought race/cultural issues were 'already included'

cell percentages

Ethnic origin	%
Black African	0
Black Caribbean	4
Indian	5
White	8
All others	8

A further category of respondent who did not mention specific proposals were those who agreed that race/cultural issues should be included, but said either that they did not know exactly how this was to be achieved or offered nothing concrete which suggested either how or why they should be included (for example 'always'), and who to all intents and purposes can be regarded as 'don't knows'. Table 8.8 shows that over a quarter of the responses from Indian respondents fell into this group, a far larger proportion than for any other group.

Table 8.8   Students who did not know how the inclusion of race/cultural issues should best be achieved

cell percentages

Ethnic origin	%
Black African	14
Black Caribbean	8
Indian	26
White	8
All others	12

Some respondents in this group adduced difficulties inherent in the process of including culture, religion, race and nationality in the curriculum:

> Being white it is difficult for me to postulate what other cultures' needs might be.

> I don't want to be taught a course featuring token blacks, Muslims etc.

Reflecting culture, religion, race and nationality in the curriculum content would also, in the view of some respondents, have a directly beneficial impact on their future working life. Table 8.9 shows that these comments came almost entirely from the white ethnic group, with over one in ten individuals believing culture etc should be included in curriculum content putting forward this argument. In stark contrast, this reason was put by not a single individual in the Black African, Black Caribbean or Indian groups.

Table 8.9   Students who thought inclusion of race/cultural issues would benefit their future work

cell percentages

Ethnic origin	%
Black African	0
Black Caribbean	0
Indian	0
White	11
All others	5

The three comments below are typical of those received in this category:

> The curriculum content should be sensitive to such issues, especially as later work life experience would be influenced by it. More so on race and nationality.

> Especially in sociology – very little time is devoted to implication of culture, race etc. and implications on treatment of ethnic minorities. This should be covered since many of the clinical placements occur within diverse inner-city hospitals.

> Different cultures will be encountered in work after this course, need to be aware of different emphasis/taboos/responses that may come up.

The reasons why respondents felt it was important to reflect culture, religion, race and nationality in the curriculum were varied, and as mentioned earlier made up the bulk of the comments received. The largest proportion of these comments stated that if they were included then they would provide socially beneficial outcomes. These focused on the increased awareness of other groups serving to promote tolerance and helping to reduce racism and dispel racist myths. Table 3.10 shows the widespread nature of this category of response, with over four in ten Black African and Black Caribbean respondents citing these, as well as over a third of white respondents.

**Table 8.10   Students who thought inclusion of race/cultural issues
to be socially beneficial**

cell percentages

Ethnic origin	%
Black African	41
Black Caribbean	46
Indian	26
White	36
All others	33

The following four responses illustrate this group of comments.
They come from respondents who categorised themselves as Black
Caribbean, White Other, White English and Malaysian respectively:

> Education destroys prejudices and gives people from all cultures an
> opportunity to learn about other cultures and therefore respect them.

> It's important that we are given different insights. In education we
> delete ignorance [and] therefore racism is less likely to occur.

> In a way that promotes two-way learning and tolerance.

> Must be able to understand and relate to other views, especially as this
> university is so mixed.

A number of respondents address themselves to how the goals of
integrating race/cultural issues into the curriculum should be
achieved. These have all been categorised as education related.
Table 8.11 shows that whilst almost half of Indian respondents
provided concrete proposals, only a little over one in ten White
respondents did so.

**Table 8.11   Students who thought inclusion of race/cultural issues
should be achieved by education-related means**

Ethnic origin	%
Black African	28
Black Caribbean	21
Indian	47
White	10
All others	38

Subsumed within this category were three major and distinct areas, these being different texts and sources, different teaching methods and perspectives and the introduction of these issues as new topics or aspects of existing courses. An example of the first of these is provided by the comments below:

> By allowing there to be more 'African' text available. Again represent-ation is always looked at but there is no identity text. (Black African student)

> More specificity of courses, most of which rely on Western texts. (White student)

The second area alluded to centred upon the beneficial impact it was believed would be made by having lecturers from ethnic minorities, who would, it was felt, provide contrasting teaching styles and fresh perspectives on courses:

> I believe that it is very important that further education should have a wide variety in teaching methods.

> It is also unfair for students from ethnic minorities to be taught from a totally Euro-centric perspective and to have their own cultural identities ignored.

Clearly these views touch upon the adequate representation of ethnic minorities among lecturers and tutors, which is an issue for all higher education institutions, as well as UEL.

Other respondents in this group stated that culture, religion, race and nationality should be directly addressed as issues, although there was a division between those who thought this should be achieved by separate modules and those who expressed the view that they should be addressed throughout courses.

QUALITATIVE RESEARCH FINDINGS

The discussion above addressed the results obtained from the questionnaire survey of staff and students which was by far the major part of the study. A smaller but nevertheless worthwhile part of the investigation was the qualitative element consisting of interviews with staff members and focus group discussions. It has to be pointed out that the focus group meetings were not well attended. The largest group at one sitting comprised just ten individuals. Four areas were covered in the discussions: expectations, perceptions, experience and association.

As far as the discussions relate to curriculum content, the majority of students felt that the institution did not meet their expectations. Their feelings about expectations were classified under three main headings:

1. future job/employment security;
2. that UEL would facilitate achievement of long-held educational hopes;
3. that they would experience a variety of cultures and gain from the experiences of others from differing backgrounds.

Students from various ethnic groups claimed that one of the attractions of the university was the diversity of culture among the student population. They expected this to be reflected in curriculum content.

In terms of experience, most students claimed that where their lecturers had included race and cultural issues, the treatment was superficial or it was done in a derogatory way. Comments about tutors included:

Narrowly focused individuals who are not culturally aware.

[They] still use words such as savages... and use materials that are offensive – they are also ignorant about the history of black achievement.

Lecturers were said to talk about black people in derogatory terms in the approach taken to discussions and that this was used to reinforce stereotypical views. One student claimed that his experience of teaching staff was consistent with his experience of individuals in other sections of the general community. He did not expect to be treated any differently:

The lecturers here are middle class white males who pretend to be politically correct... they are no different from the ordinary man in the street.

This area of discussion in the focus groups produced the liveliest responses from students. Every group discussion was favourable to the inclusion of culture, race, nationality and to a lesser extent religion, in the curriculum. Students suggested the creation of course units, the addition of black writers to the list of recommended books and the invitation of prominent ethnic minority individuals as speakers.

Black and Asian students believed that the University was missing an opportunity to exploit in a positive way the diversity of its students. They believed the University could market courses on cultural diversity and could secure funding from foreign countries who would send students to UEL.

The staff interviews covered four areas:

1. support to students;
2. communication;
3. ethnic minority staff;
4. student feedback.

The areas chosen for the interview schedule were based on analysis of the student questionnaire. The purpose of the interviews was to put to senior staff the main areas of complaint by students. Curriculum content was not covered in these interviews as the responses from students did not include it in the list of the top four major concerns.

CONCLUSION

The study at UEL found that there was enough support among both staff and students for reflecting culture, religion, race and nationality in curriculum content for UEL to give serious consideration to how it takes the issues forward. Interestingly, while not usually forming a majority, the support was broadly based and far from confined to members of ethnic minorities. Indeed, white students were often more supportive of a multicultural curriculum than some minority groups.

The staff responses, although unclear about the direction which the institution or their departments might take, nevertheless indicated commitment which the institution may well see as a foundation to build on. The response of staff was more positive than that obtained from students: 48 per cent thought that race/cultural issues should be included, and that this would be of benefit to students as well as staff.

It was clear that some departments in UEL were already reflecting these issues in curriculum content. There is, therefore, an opportunity for the sharing of knowledge across the subject area spectrum. It may be that those departments with expertise in this area could pass on their knowledge if a forum for sharing could be established.

It was clear that even among those students who thought that culture, religion, race and nationality should be reflected in the curriculum, the exact means for this process to occur were ill-defined. This would suggest that higher education institutions have a proactive role to play in this area. One method of accomplishing this would be by the setting out of concrete proposals for students to assess and provide commentary and feedback on. It could perhaps also be achieved by acting unilaterally, making changes to the curriculum and then undertaking some kind of evaluation in order to gauge whether the concerns expressed by students have in any way abated.

Throughout this process it is incumbent upon higher education institutions to be clear that it is diversity which is being addressed and not the particular concerns of any ethnic group, however vocal. The institution has to have in place appropriate methods of teaching, texts and modes of assessment which address the diversity of the student body, within which there are a host of religious, cultural, racial and national affiliations all striving for recognition, often to varying degrees. As one Black Caribbean respondent remarked in response to the question on curriculum content:

> The culture of whom? Afro-Caribbean/West Indian – difficult as no set culture. Africans varied culture – more conflict base than beneficial.

Hand-in-hand with the adoption of new teaching methods, text and modes of assessment has to be diversity within the curriculum. It would be a mistake for higher education institutions such as UEL to imagine that changes in these areas precluded any change which recognises diversity within the curriculum. Many of the staff and students' comments suggested that a more multicultural curriculum, difficult as it is to achieve, would promote tolerance, through better understanding of people.

There was a genuine belief in the need for bolstering the self-esteem and cultural identity of those from ethnic minorities, and enhancing the knowledge of non-ethnic minority students and preparing them for life in a society which is becoming increasingly culturally diverse. There is every reason to believe that this in itself would be a very laudable and worthwhile achievement, and move the institution further along the way to providing a more rounded education.

Part Three

Ethnic Stratification in Higher Education

Chapter 9

Monitoring the Progress and Achievement of Ethnic Minority Students: A New Methodology

Ruth van Dyke

This chapter aims to encourage universities to introduce a system of ethnic and gender monitoring of student progress and achievement. The discussion draws upon research conducted on the progress and achievement of ethnic minority and white students in two London universities in 1995.

The case for ethnic and gender monitoring needs to be made on two grounds. The first case for introducing ethnic monitoring is to provide a means of improving the effectiveness of higher education, and course provision in particular. While many institutions currently use course monitoring as an evaluation tool for identifying strengths and weaknesses in provision, the analysis of data on student progress and achievement is not in sufficient depth and it ignores the possibility of group variation. Institutions need to ask whether the service being delivered, which was devised with a homogeneous group of students in mind, is appropriate for the increasingly diverse student body currently occupying classrooms. Universities can begin by asking whether they are effective institutions for ethnic minority as well as white students, for women as well as men students, and for other groups who have hitherto been under-represented in higher education. This means analysing the ways in which groups of students perform and progress. It also means identifying educational policies and practices that act as barriers to the academic success of specific groups of students and modifying provision accordingly.

The second reason for introducing a system of ethnic and gender monitoring in higher education is to provide a strategy for implementing the equal opportunities policies that an increasing number of universities are devising (CUCO, 1994). Ethnic and gender monitoring provides a means of translating a university's paper commitment to equal opportunities into action. It is about using the information universities already collect on student characteristics (sex, ethnicity, age, entry qualifications) and educational outcomes (which can be taken from examination board minutes on student progress and performance) for equal opportunities purposes. Ethnic and gender monitoring can be used to:

- reveal patterns of racial/gender inequality in student progression and achievement;
- identify factors that might explain these differences;
- help devise educational policies and practices to alleviate them (CRE, 1992).

Data from the Monitoring the Progress and Achievement of Minority Ethnic Students research project will be used to illustrate the purposes highlighted above.[1]

The Monitoring the Progress and Achievement of Minority Ethnic Students research project was set up in 1994. It aimed to develop a methodology for analysing student progress and performance by ethnic group and to provide initial data on the academic outcomes of ethnic minority and white students since there was a dearth of such information. The project focused on students who were enrolled on four courses at two new London universities in 1995 and was a retrospective cohort study. Data were collected on cohorts of students who began their studies in 1991 or 1992 and who graduated in 1995. These four courses were selected because they were popular among ethnic minority students, and the data could be subjected to quantitative analysis because there were sufficient numbers of students from different ethnic groups to explore similarities and differences in performance and progress. The courses were: a social science degree, two business studies degrees and an electrical engineering degree.

The discussion that follows is structured around the key elements of ethnic monitoring: patterns of behaviour, explanatory factors and policy implications. The progress of ethnic minority and

---

1   The Monitoring the Progress and Performance of Black and Minority Ethnic Students Project was funded by RAE money at South Bank University in 1994–95. The project grew out of a discussion held by the Commission for Racial Equality Monitoring Progress Group (CREMP) which is composed of former and current equal opportunities officers in higher education and other interested academics.

white students is examined first, followed by an analysis of their performance.

PROGRESSION

There are a variety of ways of measuring student progress on degrees. The Ethnic Monitoring project focused on evidence regarding two: retention rates at the end of the first year of a degree course, as this is the crucial year for most students, and graduation rates within the normal time period. With the expansion of higher education it can no longer be assumed that students, once enrolled on a course, will 'naturally' progress to a degree. Instead universities need to ask what happens to students who embark on a course. If the retention and graduation rates of students are not deemed satisfactory then it may be necessary to devise measures to improve student progress, having first identified the barriers to specific groups of students succeeding.

Retention rates

Retention rates were measured by recording students' status at the end of the year. It was noted whether students had withdrawn from the course, transferred to another course, deferred their studies, were referred because their performance was deemed unsatisfactory or had progressed to the next year. Further differentiation was made between those who had progressed but had passed all units and those who carried a fail.

These data were used to explore several issues. Were ethnic minority and white students equally likely to progress? If not, what factors might help explain these differences and what policies might help alleviate ethnic inequalities?

Table 9.1 sets out the proportion of ethnic minority and white students who progressed from the first to second year of their degree course. It indicates that Asian students were most likely to progress and Caribbean students were least likely. Two reasons help explain most of the variation in the progress of ethnic groups. First, white, Caribbean and African students were more likely to withdraw than Asian students. More significantly, as documented in Table 9.2, Caribbean and African students were more likely to be referred.

Ruth van Dyke

**Table 9.1   Proportion of white and ethnic minority students
who progress to year two**

cell percentages

	Social science degree	Business studies 4-year degree	Business studies 3-year degree	Electrical engineering degree
White students	80.9	84.2	58.9	66.7
Asian students	94.4	88.0	70.6	100.0
Caribbean students	66.6	66.7*	25.0	100.0**
African students	86.9	64.3	46.7	81.8

*   Only three Caribbean students were identified in this cohort
**   Only two Caribbean students were identified from student records in this cohort.
However there were nine students whose ethnic status was unknown, thus it is
possible that there were more Caribbean students on the course.

**Table 9.2   Proportion of students who were referred in first year
units or were required to repeat the first year,
by ethnic group**

cell percentages

	Social science degree	Business studies 4-year degree	Business studies 3-year degree	Electrical engineering degree
White students	3.2	13.2	26.4	6.7
Asian students	5.6	12.0	29.4	0.0
Caribbean students	10.3	33.3*	50.0	0.0
African students	4.3	35.7	40.0	0.0

*   Only three Caribbean students were identified in this cohort.

Student progress has become an important educational issue. It is a
Higher Education Quality Assurance assessment target. It has
financial implications for universities. It is also a measure of equality
of opportunity within higher education. Higher education institutions, therefore, may need to take action if ethnic and gender monitoring reveals patterns of inequality.

The findings from the Ethnic Monitoring project suggest that
strategies targeted at weak students might have a profound effect on
the progress of black students. Educational practices that might
promote minority group progress include: pre-entry preparation
classes; first year units that help bridge differences in students'

knowledge base, study skills courses, language and mathematics support classes and a strong personal tutorial system for first year students. Tighter admissions criteria might also need to be considered so the pressure to fill student target numbers does not set up some groups of students to fail. These are the kind of initiatives that American universities have instituted during the past ten years in order to recruit and retain African Americans in higher education (see, for example, Office of Minority Affairs, 1991; Lang and Ford, 1998).

The figures in Table 9.1 suggest that progression to the second year is not an issue for the majority of students in each ethnic group. However, some students were progressed carrying a condoned fail. Caribbean and African students were more likely than white and Asian students to progress carrying a fail. While the decision by the examinations board to progress students carrying a fail might be seen as beneficial to students who are not held back due to their unsatisfactory performance on one unit, such practices may actually jeopardise these students' academic success if they are subsequently left to their own devices. An academic support structure specifically aimed at students who are identified as weak at examination boards should enhance students' performance in their second and final years. Such structures would particularly benefit Caribbean and African students.

A second crucial measure of student progress is graduation rates. Were ethnic minority and white groups equally likely to achieve a degree? Differences in graduation rates between ethnic groups might suggest that universities were not operating in a way that helped equalise life chances but in ways that helped reinforce stratification on ethnic/racial grounds.

Graduation within normal time period

Data from the four courses studied indicate that there are significant differences in the graduation rates of different ethnic groups. For example, Table 9.3 shows that the graduation rates for social science students ranged from 43 per cent for Caribbeans to 87 per cent for Asians. On the engineering degree none of the African students completed their degree in the normal time period compared to 63 per cent of Asian students.

Table 9.3   Graduation rate by course and ethnic group

cell percentages

	Social science degree	Business studies 4-year degree	Business studies 3-year degree	Electrical engineering degree
White students	61.9	65.4	13.5**	31.3
Asian students	86.9	59.3	23.5**	62.5
Caribbean students	43.6	66.7*	0.0	0.0
African students	60.9	44.4	26.7**	0.0

*   There were only 3 Caribbean students in the original cohort.
**   7 white students, 3 Asian students and 1 African student from the 1992 cohort
     decided to do a placement at the end of their second year which in part accounts
     for the small proportion of students graduating.

While the percentage graduating may be seen as low for all students
and hence is recognisable as a problem for universities in terms of
quality assurance, ethnic group variations require particular consideration. Already it is clear that the high referral rates in the first
year help account for the smaller proportion of Caribbean and African
students who obtain a degree qualification in the normal time span of
their course. Poor performance in their second year leading to
referral is another barrier that Caribbean and African students are
more likely to face.

A limitation of the cohort study was that the outcomes for the
students who were referred in their first or second year were not
investigated. Thus there was no information which indicates whether
students who were referred fall by the wayside or whether they take
longer to obtain a degree but get there in the end. Universities that
have adopted a more flexible approach to learning, which allows
students to progress at their own rate, might be enhancing the
academic success of its students as measured by their graduation
rates over a longer time span: four or five years instead of the normal
three.

A number of changes in the higher education system, in particular
in degree structure and in the student grant, may be affecting study
patterns and thus the period in which degrees are completed. To
obtain a more accurate picture of student progress would thus
require collection of data on graduation rates over several years,
periods, a practice which is currently undertaken in the United
States.

However, based on the evidence at hand, the lower graduation rates of Caribbean and African students suggest a wastage of potential from these communities. Moreover, it means that universities are continuing to help reproduce racial inequalities in society, particularly in terms of access to university qualifications and subsequent graduate job opportunities.

Analysing student retention and graduation is one means of measuring the effectiveness and equality of opportunity of higher education. However, it is also important to evaluate performance.

Student achievement

Previous studies on student achievement (mostly looking at achievement by sex or entry qualifications) have focused almost exclusively on degree results (Clarke, 1988; Bourner and Hamed, 1987; Page et al, 1994; McCrum, 1995). However, such analysis gives only a partial picture of performance and it is limited in its ability to determine factors that might contribute to student success and failure. In contrast, the 1995 research project examined four measures of student achievement: mean marks for coursework in each unit, mean marks for exams in each unit and the mean mark for the unit as a whole, and degree results.

The range of data the Ethnic Monitoring project collected highlighted differences in performance in relation to type of assessment or units where some students performed particularly poorly or well. In addition it exposed patterns of discrimination since the researchers heard allegations of discrimination in marking in assignments that were not anonymously marked. For example:

> So and so never gives black students above a 55.

> I helped a white student with an assignment and when we got them back he asked me what I got. He got an A and I got a C. He couldn't believe it.

Ethnic minority students' allegations of racism in marking have got to be taken seriously because educational practices, like non-anonymously marked assignments, provide an opportunity for individual prejudice to express itself. Comprehensive ethnic monitoring could be a method of revealing bias in marking practices.

In all four courses studied, white and Asian students' performance was higher than Caribbean and African students. For a number of units white and Asian students obtained marks that were significantly higher than Caribbean and African students; in most cases there was six to twelve points difference or a difference in class of mark.

On some courses a distinct hierarchy of ethnic performance was established during the first year and carried on throughout the course or most of the course. Thus Asian students had higher marks than white and African students throughout the engineering degree. On the four year business studies degree white students achieved the highest marks in the first and second years; but, by the final year, Asian students were obtaining comparable marks.

On the social science and three-year business studies degree there were a number of changes in the performance of ethnic groups across the course. On the social science degree Asian students emerged as marginally more successful than white, Caribbean and African students who had comparable marks in the first year. But in the second year the marks of African students were distinctly lower than those obtained by other groups of students and in the third year both Caribbean and African students were achieving significantly lower marks, particularly on units assessed by examinations.

On the three-year business studies course there were more dramatic shifts in ethnic group performance. In the first year the achievement hierarchy was topped by Asian students followed by white students, with African students having the lowest performance. But in the second year white students were most successful and Asian students slipped to the bottom.

What does this information on ethnic group achievement tell us? First, these data challenge the stereotype that white students perform best in higher education. Asian students' levels of academic achievement along with their lower withdrawal rates and higher completion rates suggest that as a group they can be more successful than white students in the new universities. Secondly, the results suggest that progression rates may affect group achievement. In the case of the four courses studied, white, Caribbean and African students were more likely to withdraw from the course or be referred compared to Asian students. As a result, a smaller proportion of weak or uncommitted students from these groups may progress compared to Asian students, with consequences for group performance in the second and third years. Changes in group achievement across the course also suggest that some groups are less likely to acquire the skills to undertake more advanced work or are unaware of the requirements of the course at more advanced levels. The implication of this latter finding is that courses are not equally effective for students from different ethnic groups.

Differences in staff-student interaction may account for some of this variability and will be discussed in greater depth later in this chapter.

However, the data also document ethnic inequalities. How can these differences be explained? What factors might enhance or undermine the achievement of groups of students? To address these questions several sources of information were considered. Relevant literature from Britain and from the United States was consulted. Focus groups with ethnic minority and white students and student parents were organised to find out what factors students felt hampered or enhanced their performance. Finally, a student questionnaire was devised and distributed in order to obtain information about factors the researchers felt might be pertinent to student performance: parental status; responsibility for caring for other dependants; English as first language; employment patterns during the course; and experience of homelessness during the course. However, it proved impossible to examine the relationship between these factors and student performance because insufficient numbers of questionnaires were obtained from three of the cohorts of students studied. The large numbers of students who did not progress on these courses, combined with the timing of the questionnaire distribution at the end of the academic year, deterred data collection. Nevertheless, information acquired from the other methods suggests that four factors might contribute to ethnic differences in achievement: type of learning assessment, English language proficiency, curriculum and staff-student interaction. Each of these factors will be discussed along with their policy implications.

Type of learning assessment

A key factor that contributes to the poorer performance of ethnic minority students on some courses is their significantly lower marks on examinations. Moreover, good or satisfactory standards of achievement on course work can be masked by very poor performances on exams. For example, Table 9.4 highlights the marks groups of students were awarded on two units of the three-year business studies degree.

It is clear from this evidence that African students' course work was of a high standard, and in fact they were meeting the assessment criteria to a higher standard than white students. However, the answers they produced for examinations were of a poor standard, and much worse than those of white students. Ethnic minority students' final unit marks suggest a much poorer performance than white students because of the extra loading given to examinations. The traditional higher education practice of assessment weighted towards exams therefore might not be 'neutral'. The evidence suggests that this assessment regime has a more adverse effect on ethnic minority students' achievement than white students.

Table 9.4   Mean marks (%) for two second year units on the three-year business studies degree

| | Management accounting | | | Human resource management | | |
	Unit	Coursework	Exam	Unit	Coursework	Exam
White students	53.9	64.6	49.9	55.5	57.8	54.3
Asian students	45.7	64.0	39.5	43.3	47.9	41.5
African students	48.9	70.9	37.6	53.4	60.1	43.1

How can differences in examination performance be explained? Caribbean and African students may find examinations a bigger hurdle than other students because they tend to be older as a group and thus are less likely to have recent exam practice. Moreover, they may not be clear about what knowledge and skills a university examination will be testing or, as Gallagher et al (1993) found, they may have less confidence in performing this task. However, even when Caribbean and African students are in the traditional age bracket (18–19 years old) examinations may be problematic because Cheryl Gore's research (1996) suggests that they are less likely, as a group, to have acquired good exam revision skills, than white students, because they are more likely to have attended schools in inner city areas where there was inadequate preparation in examination techniques.[2]

While examinations are an important barrier to academic success of ethnic minority students, they may also compound obstacles for a group for students who are defined by their entry qualifications rather than their ethnicity. As set out in Table 9.5, *all* students with

2   Cheryl Gore investigated the ethnic composition of 'effective' schools. She also looked at the educational practices in 'effective' and 'less effective schools' that might have produced differences in examination achievement. Her findings imply that less effective schools did not adequately train their pupils to take examinations. I have thus argued that students who attended less effective schools will not be able to draw on good exam preparation skills in higher education. They will be less well equipped to cope with university assessment practices.

Access qualifications (white and ethnic minority) performed significantly worse on examinations than students with A-levels on the social science degree. This finding complements Langridge's small-scale study (1993) which indicated that Access students perform less well on examinations and suggests that the results from this form of assessment do not reflect the students' true ability.

Table 9.5   Mean exam mark (%) for psychology year one, social science degree

	Students with A-level qualifications (12+ points)	Students with Access qualifications
White students	57.7	44.7
Asian students	55.4	47.5
Caribbean students	53.8	43.5
African students	56.0	47.1

However, these differences in performance have a disproportionate effect on the group achievement of Caribbean and African students since Access courses are a more important route of entry to higher education for them than for white and Asian students. Of the student cohort who took the psychology exam, more than half the black students came via the Access route compared to 20 per cent of white and Asian students. This evidence tells us that examinations as a form of assessment present a higher barrier to ethnic minority students than white students.

This example of ethnic monitoring of student achievement revealed patterns of racial inequality and identified an obstacle – preparedness for examinations – that might account for some of the differences between ethnic groups. The Commission for Racial Equality's position is that this type of information should be used to inform the policy-making process and in particular should be used to develop strategies to alleviate ethnic differences.

There are four policy options that could be considered to tackle ethnic differences in examination performance. They are:

1. The institution takes no action. It could be argued that this option is in breach of the spirit of the Race Relations Act 1976. Such a response ignores the increasing diversity among the university student body and therefore the necessity of varying modes of assessment to reflect students' different learning styles.

2. Another policy option would be for admissions staff to identify the Access courses that feed into the institution and to work with tutors on devising strategies to enhance the exam preparedness of Access students. This would benefit all Access students but would not help other groups of ethnic minority students who are performing poorly on examinations.
3. A third option would be to organise exam preparation sessions centrally or departmentally for undergraduate students and/or devise mock examinations and feedback sessions as part of the learning strategy within each subject area.
4. The final strategy is a review of the range and weighting of assessments on undergraduate courses. The assessment regime could be altered if there is an over reliance on testing the skills assessed by examination. A widening of the range of assessments would benefit all students as a greater range of skills would be tested. Such changes would be of particular benefit to some groups of ethnic minority students who appear to be disadvantaged by traditional assessment practices.

While the evidence demonstrates that examinations present higher barriers to academic success for some groups of students than others, additional research needs to be undertaken to examine the way groups of students prepare for exams and to look for group variations in the way students answer exam questions. English language proficiency might help explain some of the ethnic exam variation.

Proficiency in standard English

Proficiency in standard English is the second factor that might explain variation in ethnic group achievement in higher education.

A variety of initiatives in the 1980s highlighted the importance of language in educational achievement (Robson, 1988; ILEA, 1989, 1990). A recent project at the University of North London (UNL) has built on the work undertaken in secondary, further and adult education. The Language and Learning Project at UNL was part of a Higher Education Funding Council for England (HEFCE) funded initiative to increase the participation and the academic success of ethnic minority students in Initial Teacher Training (Neophytou et al, 1995). The project was based on the notion that standard English is not the first language for many people. The project showed that bilingual students and speakers of Caribbean Creole need to develop awareness of their own language patterns and the differences between it and standard English in order to learn the 'language currency of higher education'. To facilitate the acquisition of English language skills the Language and Learning Project ran staff workshops to identify the linguistic requirements of the course and to make these requirements explicit. It also offered a range of language workshops which were open to all students. The language transition these workshops promoted, and consequently the academic success fostered, is demonstrated in the following comment made by one bilingual student:

> Getting advice and guidance with the expressions to use in order to lay out my essay was useful. Also being made aware of the differences between English and Bengali and how this influenced my writing, I was able to proof read my work for errors I made. This meant I passed and got better grades, which was very pleasing. (Neophytou et al, 1995)

It may be that, as ethnic minority students become more acquainted with the language requirements of higher education, the gap in marks between white and ethnic ethnic students is reduced. On the other hand, if course provision and student feedback do not make the linguistic requirements of the course explicit and students are not aware of their linguistic weakness, the gap in achievement may widen as they progress and marking becomes tougher.

There are several policy implications that emanate from this finding. Firstly it suggests that universities should review their language policies and support systems. They may want to look at the evidence accumulating from projects like the Language and Learning Project at UNL as well as those in further and adult education and to consider how it might help improve the performance of their students. Secondly, that HEFCE may need to alter the way in which it distributes resources to universities. It may want to allocate additional money for language workshops to universities (likely to be former polytechnics) who enrol a large number of students for whom standard English is not their first language. In order to provide equality of opportunity, that is equality of access and participation to all students, HEFCE will need to acknowledge the diversity of students' backgrounds and experiences and enable universities to cater for these differences (HEFCE, 1996). Finally, it has repercussions for the work of academics. They may need to spend more time considering the linguistic requirements of the units they teach and the course as a whole in order to help make them explicit and in order to devise strategies to ensure *all* students can acquire the requisite skills.

But at the same time universities as a whole need to consider whether too great an emphasis is placed on the style of presentation rather than on the content of students' work. Ethnic minority students, who participated in focus group interviews for the Ethnic Monitoring project, made the case that the ability to communicate in 'white'/standard English was a factor that enhanced academic success. They made the following comments:

> I feel that we should be marked according to the content, not according to our writing styles, because we come from different backgrounds... I thought it was an economics assignment, not an English assignment. It's not that we want extra favours. It's just that my writing style is a bit different from an English guy, my expressions are different, and I want them to mark me on my facts, not my writing style. So I feel that, that is the main reason why we are penalised... But we are different and it has to be taken into account that we are different.

> It's like this oral exam we've got now for Business Policy. I tell you I'm not being pessimistic but a lot of black people are not going to do well because they expect us to speak good English grammar, yeah. The way you approach everything is got to be different from the way a white person is going to put their [ideas]... because we have different backgrounds, you know; and it's a second language too.

These comments made by two groups of students on two different courses at two different institutions suggest that a particular kind of written and oral English plays an important role in the marks students are awarded by academic staff. They also indicate that ethnic minority students are less likely to have the English styles that are considered appropriate, and as a result they are likely to achieve lower marks than white students. There is a feeling that the criteria that are being applied are discriminatory, because they are imbedded in white culture and because there is no recognition of the language skills these students have to offer.

According to the evidence, English language skills and marking criteria with respect to written and oral language styles are important factors that might account for some of the variation in ethnic group achievement. As mentioned, they have a number of policy implications for higher education institutions, not least a challenge to the way in which white middle class academics set criteria that are exclusionary.

The curriculum is the third factor that may help explain ethnic differences in student achievement.

Curriculum

The curriculum may enhance or inhibit the academic success of ethnic minority students. Data from two units on the social science and business studies degree illustrate this argument.

Data from the social science degree revealed one very interesting anomaly. On just one unit, Developing Societies, all ethnic minority groups achieved higher mean marks than white students. A likely hypothesis is that the subject matter of this unit was of particular interest to ethnic minority students. As a result they did more work (reading, discussing, etc) for this unit than white students. A curriculum that is less Eurocentric may therefore have an important effect on the academic success of students who are studying in the social sciences and humanities.

However, the content of the Quantitative Methods units on both the business studies degrees had the opposite effect as Caribbean and African students were likely to fail this unit. This unit epitomises the way in which one element of a course can act as a significant barrier to student achievement and progression. There are a range of policy options that could be considered to alleviate ethnic inequalities in achievement in this subject: provide a pre-entry bridging course, mathematics support classes, review the unit and reconsider the mathematics requirements of the course.

This evidence indicates that ethnic monitoring by unit is a useful tool for highlighting areas of success as well as barriers to student progress.

Staff–student interaction

The last factor to be considered is staff–student interaction. A number of studies, conducted in the United States, document the importance of academic–student contact in promoting student achievement (Nettles, 1988; Allen, 1992; Kobrack, 1992). For example, Nettles (1988) found 'generally, students who have frequent contact with faculty outside the classroom receive higher grades'. He went on to say, 'black students have significantly less contact with faculty outside the classroom than white students and this contributes to the lower grades for black students', a finding substantiated in other studies (Allen, 1992).

This research suggests that a positive relationship between student achievement and academic interaction exists in British universities, and that, as in the United States, ethnic minority students are less likely than white students to have frequent/positive contacts with the predominantly white academic staff. Differences in staff–student interaction would thus account for some of the variation in ethnic group achievement.

There are several ways that staff–student interaction may be more beneficial to white students than ethnic minority students. First, white academic staff may hold stereotypical views about the academic potential of students based on their ethnicity. Certainly, some ethnic minority students believe staff have lower expectations of them than of white students. For example, as a student in one focus group interview commented:

> On this particular course they've already chosen who will get the first class degree and it's a white person that I know... and the others will probably just get 2.1s and the majority of black people, I feel, will get, specially those who come from the African continent, 2.2s or thirds and it seems like that [outcome] will be determined from the time you start your second year... And that's what I'm finding with this particular college... But I do have a friend at another university that is experiencing a similar situation to this... And you know, there doesn't seem to be anything that you can do about it and you just sort of go home in tears.

There is evidence that expectations have an effect on students' academic performance (Kobrack, 1992). It may be that ethnic minority students become demotivated; that they may become unwilling to do their best if they are not going to obtain a mark commensurate with their efforts. Their poorer performance, in turn, may then help to reinforce the stereotypes held by academic staff. This finding suggests that additional research needs to be undertaken to look at actual, albeit possibly hidden, expectations that academics hold of the academic potential of students from different ethnic groups. Armed with this additional data it may be possible for universities to consider measures to challenge and alter racist stereotypes held by staff which hamper the academic performance of ethnic minority students and undermine the institution's equal opportunities policy.

Secondly, ethnic minority students, Caribbean and African in particular, may have less contact with academic staff and as a result get less information and less feedback on their work than white students. Focus group discussions revealed that 'knowing the rules of the game' is one of the factors that enhanced students' academic performance. In part, students learn the rules of the game from academic staff. Ethnic minority students may pick up these rules more slowly and often when it is too late. After they have handed in their coursework, they may learn that the rules (that is the assessment criteria or expectations) have changed as the student has progressed on the course.

It seems one of the 'rules of the game' is about getting plenty of feedback about ideas and coursework from staff. As one black student put it:

> But then you know, you do have certain people who understand what I can only call the 'rules of the game'. That they should take everything not just to one lecturer but to two, three or four lecturers. And you know, if they can get a couple of home numbers, they're really in there.

There was a strong perception that white students are in a better position than ethnic minority students to play this game. Ethnic minority students felt that some staff responded more positively to overtures from white students. In addition, it is clear from evidence presented earlier in this chapter, and from the focus group interviews, that ethnic minority students also experienced racism and this affected relationships between staff and students.

> One day I actually overheard X make racist comments about us to another lecturer. X said there were too many Africans in [the university] and that we were all dumb fools.

This kind of remark will get transmitted through the student grapevine and is likely to affect the way the group responds to members of staff. These staff may no longer be perceived as 'helpful' to black students. While such explicit racist remarks may be unusual, ethnic minority students may be more likely to judge staff who are unhelpful as 'racist' because of their previous experience of racism, particularly in schools. As a result of these varied experiences more academic staff may be deemed 'out of bounds' to ethnic minority students than to white students.

More research needs to be done in this area to understand what role staff–student interaction plays in generating variations in ethnic achievement. Meanwhile, academic staff need to consider how their behaviour may have an impact on student performance.

CONCLUSION

This initial analysis of data on the progress and achievement of groups of students demonstrates the value of ethnic monitoring to higher education institutions. Ethnic monitoring can aid the quality assurance process as it provides additional data about the effectiveness of course-specific and university-wide educational practices on specific groups of students. In addition, it has an important role to play in promoting equality of opportunity in service delivery, which an increasing number of universities subscribe to, at least on paper.

The evidence that emerged from this project indicates that individual merit may not be the only defining variable that influences student progress and performance. Ethnic group variation suggests that universities are not effective institutions for all groups of students. Ethnic minorities appear to have more barriers to success than white students. Many of these obstacles relate to institutional practices. The data suggest that higher education institutions are not practising equality of opportunity in service delivery. Moreover, the smaller proportion of Caribbean and African students who complete their degrees and their lower degree awards will adversely affect their labour market position. Universities, therefore, may be reinforcing racial stratification in society rather than helping to remedy it.

The Higher Education Statistical Agency requirement that all universities collect ethnicity data on students enrolled on higher education courses means that ethnic monitoring is a feasible practice. Universities have the data necessary, they now need to make the commitment to analysing it and acting on the findings.

Walter Allen, an academic involved in studying the experience of African Americans in higher education, testifies to the value of ethnic monitoring when he states that universities must

> ...map out and understand the complex relationships that culminate in so few blacks qualifying for, entering and completing college. Having done so, [universities] can then target places where intervention could yield positive results. Such an approach would be preferable to any response suggesting that universities are unable to address key factors that influence black students' college attendance and graduation... (Allen, 1992)

And James Duderstadt, the former President of the University of Michigan, highlights the context of diversity, equality of opportunity and academic excellence that ethnic and gender monitoring needs to be imbedded in. In the Michigan Mandate, which sets out the vision of the future, he stated:

> For the University to achieve excellence in teaching and research in the years ahead, for it to serve our state, our nation, and the world, we simply must achieve and sustain a campus community recognised for its

racial and ethnic diversity. But beyond this, we believe that the University has a mandate... to build a model of pluralistic, multicultural community for our nation.

In this effort it is clear that a fundamental purpose of the Michigan Mandate must be to remove all institutional barriers to full participation in the life of the University and the educational opportunities it offers to people of all races, creeds, ethnic groups. (Dunderstadt, 1990)

Chapter 10

Failure of Asian Students in Clinical Examinations: The Manchester Experience

Aneez Esmail and Paul Dewart[1]

The extent of racial disadvantage in the UK has been well documented (Modood et al, 1997) and recent work by Modood and colleagues (Modood and Shiner 1994) has also highlighted the disadvantage faced by ethnic minorities as they try to gain access to higher education. Traditionally, ethnic minority applicants to medicine have always been over-represented when compared to the proportion in the general population (Vellins, 1982). However, the racial mix of the applicants to medical schools is almost exclusively made up of applicants who classify themselves as Indians, with applicants who classify themselves as Bangladeshi, Pakistani and Afro-Caribbean being under-represented when compared to their proportions in the general population (Esmail et al, 1996). Perhaps because of the large number of Asian students in British medical schools, there is a perception that discrimination is not a factor in selection or in the examination success of students. Just as, because nearly 30 per cent of the medical staff is classified by the Department of Health as ethnic minorities (NHSE, 1997), there is also a perception that somehow the medical profession itself was immune from

1   We would like to acknowledge the support of the Dean of Manchester University Medical School, Professor Stephen Tomlinson, for allowing us to publish the data and for his comments on earlier drafts of the chapter. Roger Green, Dean for Undergraduate Studies, and John McClure, Dean for Undergraduate Examinations, also provided helpful comments. Aneez Esmail would also like to thank The Commonwealth Fund of New York whose financial support during his tenure as Harkness Fellow 1997–1998 enabled him to write the paper.

the problems of discrimination which have been documented for the general population in employment, schooling and higher education.

That racial bias is a factor in the career progress of ethnic minority doctors has been documented by Esmail and colleagues (Esmail and Everington, 1993, 1997) and highlighted in a recent report by the Commission for Racial Equality (CRE, 1996). Esmail and McManus (Esmail et al, 1994; McManus et al, 1989) have also suggested that racial bias is probably operating in the selection policies of some medical schools. Ethnic minority doctors are more likely to be disciplined by the General Medical Council (Esmail and Everington, 1994) compared to white doctors. They continue to be under-represented in the professional organisations of the medical profession and are also less likely to be rewarded in terms of career progress and remuneration. Much of this evidence suggests that the medical profession is not immune from the problems of racial discrimination. However, what distinguishes the medical profession from some professional groups is its failure to recognise the problem of discrimination within its own structures and take steps to deal with it (Esmail and Carnall, 1997; though see Singh, Chapter 11 in this book, on universities in this respect).

Higher education establishments responsible for the training of doctors are also susceptible to the charge that they discriminate against ethnic minorities. The problems related to selection of students for medical school have already been highlighted (Esmail et al, 1994, 1996; McManus et al, 1989). Another area where there is growing concern among students and lecturers is the role of discrimination in exam success. Whilst most medical colleges and universities have now instituted systems for the anonymous marking of written papers or multiple choice questionnaires, the need to examine the clinical competence of medical students in face to face examinations opens up the possibility of discrimination which may not be apparent in courses which assess students predominantly by anonymously marked exams. There is considerable suspicion among lecturers and students at some medical schools that ethnic minority students may have a higher failure rate in clinical examinations compared to their white colleagues. The absence of systematic monitoring of the performance of ethnic minority students either in the application process for medical school entry or the progress of students once admitted makes it difficult to assess whether there is any factual basis for this suspicion.

This chapter describes the experience of one medical school as it sought an explanation as to why all ten students who failed their clinical examinations in 1994 were Asian. It describes a simple method of assessing whether the failure rate was statistically significant and discusses some of the issues that were raised as a result of the analysis.

THE MEDICAL CURRICULUM AND ASSESSMENT PROCEDURES IN MANCHESTER

The medical curriculum in Manchester is undergoing radical restructuring, but for the period in question (1989–1994) the curriculum was fairly traditional, based on a five-year course. Performance of students was assessed by written examinations in the first three years of the curriculum and by a combination of written and clinical examinations in the final two years. There was no system of monitoring of ethnicity or gender in place although there were concerns about the failure and drop out rate of students on the medical course. The possibility of racial bias influencing exam success was first raised when the results of the final examinations in 1994 showed that all ten students who failed were Asian students. Following advice from several individuals including one of the authors, the Dean ordered an investigation into the results of this examination to determine whether this was a chance finding or the possibility of some systematic bias.

Analysis of the failure rate of students

The first problem that had to be addressed was whether the exam results in 1994 were an aberration which only became apparent because all the students who failed were Asian or whether it was part of a trend which had been present for some time. In the absence of any data on the ethnicity and gender of the students, it was decided that names would be used to determine both the ethnicity and gender of the students. Whilst this has obvious problems and would almost certainly misclassify some students, it was felt that it would be specific enough to classify the majority of students, particularly since the vast majority of ethnic minority students were Asian.

A retrospective analysis of the achievement records in written and clinical examinations of the medical students taking their final exams in 1994, throughout the five-year course, was carried out. A total of 228 who sat their Final MBChB examinations in June 1994 were identified and divided into groups according to ethnicity and gender determined by their name. Using this method, 134 students were male with 40 having names suggesting that they were from ethnic minorities and 94 were female, 20 with names suggestive of being from an ethnic minority. Students whose names were not suggestive of being from an ethnic minority will be referred to as European.

Results

Analysis of the first and second-year exams where there is no face-to-face contact between examiner and student showed that there was no significant difference in results between ethnic minority students and European students or between males and females. Similarly, in the third year written examinations there were no significant differences overall but European students achieved higher marks in pathology and microbiology. This was not investigated further.

With respect to the Final MB examination, ethnic minority students were twice as likely to fail the fourth-year clinical examination compared to their European colleagues. This difference was statistically significant ($p=0.02$). All ten students who failed the Final MB exam were from an ethnic minority group ($p<0.01$). Where there was a written component to the examinations, there was no difference in performance between ethnic minorities and European students. A similar proportion of honours degrees were awarded to ethnic minority and European students.

The results of the Final MB examination in 1994 are shown in Table 10.1. The examination is divided into three parts. Part 1 consists of the clinical subjects of medicine, surgery, obstetrics, paediatrics and psychiatry. Public Health is also included in this section but is not a clinical exam. All subjects in Part 1 have a clinical component with the student being required to take part in a face to face examination with a clinical examiner. Public Health is a written exam with only a small part of the marks being attributable to the oral. The table shows the maximum number of marks for each examination, the mean score achieved for each examination by European students and ethnic minority students and the standard deviation of the scores. The differences between the two scores have been assessed using the unpaired t test. The results show that for all exams except obstetrics, psychiatry and public health in Part 1 of the Final MB examination, ethnic minority students scored significantly lower marks than their colleagues with European names.

Table 10.1   Final MB exams; comparison of ethnic minority and European named students

| Examination | Max | Anglo-Saxon (n=168) | | Ethnic minority (n=60) | | |
		Mean	SD	Mean	SD	unpaired
Part 1						
Medicine	(20)	14.8	3.1	12.5	3.1	p<0.001
Surgery	(20)	14.5	2.98	12.8	3.9	p<0.001
Obstetrics	(20)	13.16	2.45	12.53	2.14	p=0.078
Paediatrics	(20)	13.66	2.64	12.27	2.53	p<0.001
Psychiatry	(20)	13.93	2.58	13.13	2.24	p=0.035
Public health	(20)	14.45	2.6	14.33	3.1	p=0.775
Part 2						
Research SSM or						
Revision SSM	(30)	22.5	3.87	20	5.25	p<0.001
Part 3						
Clinical SSM	(20)	16.5	1.4	15.9	1.78	p<0.001
Final papers	(60)	33.12	13.14	33.5	5.09	p=0.631
Overall total		156.7	13.4	146.4	18.3	p<0.001

In Part 2 of the Final MB examination, students carry out a research project working closely with a supervisor. The Research SSM (Special Study Module) is a written paper and is marked by the supervisor and independently by one external examiner who usually has had no contact with the student. The marks are derived from the average of the two scores given by the supervisor and the independent external examiner. The results in Table 10.1 show that it was the only written examination where there was a difference between the two groups of students.

In Part 3 of the exam, the Final Papers are written exams and the results show that there was no difference in the mean scores of European and ethnic minority students. The Clinical SSM is assessed in a similar manner to the Research SSM and involves considerable interaction between the supervisor and the student.

Analysis of the differences in gender is not tabulated, but overall, female students scored higher marks in clinical examinations (average score of males = 16.11; average score of females 16.7 p=0.04). A difference of 0.4 represents a 4 per cent difference in marks and could be important to a candidate who is borderline. There were no gender differences in the marks for written examinations. Asian female students performed as well as the white students in clinical examinations and there were no statistical differences between Asian female students and white students.

DISCUSSION

The findings tabulated and presented above confirm that the differences in final examinations observed between ethnic minority and European students was not a chance finding. Although the methods of identification of ethnicity and gender were principally by interpretation of name and not declared by the student, any bias resulting from this was likely to reduce the differences and therefore can be discounted. For example, Afro-Caribbean and Christian Indians would be classified as having European names and hence tend to minimise the differences between the two groups. That all ten students who failed the final MB examination were Asian is corroborated by the examination committee.

The differences in average scores between European students and ethnic minority students, although small, point to the fact that there is a systematic difference between the two groups of students, suggesting that it is these differences which probably accounted for the fact that all ten students who failed the exam were Asian. These differences were only apparent in examinations where there was a clinical/face-to-face component or where there was a lot of interaction between a supervisor and student. The findings raise several important questions about the possibility of racial bias, the conduct of clinical examinations and the future monitoring of the performance of students.

Differences could have occurred for several reasons. It could be argued that the attitude of ethnic minority students towards the final examination was more complacent than their white colleagues. There is a perception among some medical educators that many Asian students are forced into studying medicine through family pressures. They are not therefore as committed to the discipline as their white colleagues or alternatively they study in a different manner. For example, a senior examiner stated a commonly held view that Asian students 'tend to hit the books' and might be good theoretically but not clinically. Such attitudes, although anecdotal, are not uncommon and conform to a racial stereotype of Asian students.

The issue of communication and rapport with their patients is sometimes raised as a possibility to account for the differences between clinical and written examination skills. All the Asian students who failed were British students, who had gone through the British education system and therefore were fluent in English. Why they should be any different from their white colleagues cannot be easily explained.

The issue is further complicated by the fact that all the Asian students who failed were male. Asian female students did just as well as their white colleagues in the clinical examinations. If the reason for the failure of Asian students was because of possible discrimination, then we need to understand why it was only restricted to male students. The racial stereotypes described above are not just restricted to male students and it is difficult to argue that racial discrimination is only restricted to male Asian students. Paradoxically, Collier and Burke (1986) showed that ethnic minority women were more disadvantaged than their male colleagues when applying to medical schools, but there is little research on gender differences and discrimination in exam success in higher education. Within the Manchester cohort, the small numbers of ethnic minority women make sub-group analysis meaningless. It is beyond the scope of this discussion to explain why these differences may have occurred but they should be taken into account in any discussion of this complex issue.

Clinical examinations involve a complex interaction between student, patient and examiner which is poorly understood. The patient may not like the student and therefore make it difficult for the student to take a history. Patients are chosen from a pool of patients attending hospitals and it may be a possibility that this could be a factor in individual cases. However, it would be highly unlikely that all ten students who failed had the misfortune to get patients who for example did not like Asians and therefore made it difficult for them to take a history. Asian students may of course be at an advantage if the patient they were allocated was Asian and spoke the same language as them.

The attitude of the examiner towards the student is also important. Clinical examiners are usually volunteers and most are NHS consultants. Whilst they are specialists within their own field, they are usually not teachers in the common understanding of the term. At present, in Manchester, there is no formal mechanism of ensuring that examiners are trained to examine and a large element of subjectivity may be involved in making a decision about the competency of the student. If the examiner is racially biased, then there is at present no means of monitoring this and excluding such examiners from the examination process. Whilst discrimination at this level may not be overt, the fact that it could exist has been suggested by research carried out by Esmail and Everington (1993, 1997). If NHS consultants show racial bias in the selection of doctors for junior hospital posts then there is no reason to assume that bias does not exist in a clinical examination.

Medical school entrants tend to score above average marks in their A-level results and ethnic minority entrants are similar to their white colleagues in this respect. In fact white students have a greater chance of being admitted to medical school with lower grades then their ethnic minority colleagues (Esmail et al, 1996). The possibility that the higher failure rate of ethnic minority students is because they were not of the same academic ability can therefore be excluded.

The fact that there was no difference in performance between ethnic minority students and European students in the first three years of the curriculum where exams are marked anonymously is important. Differences only arose in face to face clinical examinations and the possibility of racial bias being a factor is therefore compelling.

POLICY IMPLICATIONS

It is fair to state that the authorities in Manchester were surprised by the findings. However, to their credit, they made the findings public and instituted a process of far-reaching reforms to the examination process. From September 1995, all students registering with the Faculty of Medicine were asked to voluntarily declare their ethnicity using a set of questions similar to those employed in the census. This will enable future monitoring of results to take place and will no longer be dependent on using the name of the candidate as a proxy for ethnicity and gender. In the analysis of examination results, monitoring of performance by ethnicity and gender will now become routine.

Clinical examinations, by their nature, are very subjective and it has long been accepted by medical educators that they are not a good measure of a students ability. In the traditional face-to-face clinical examination, a student is usually asked to examine a patient either in front of an examiner or to report the findings of the examination to an examiner. There is no objective measure of what is expected of the student and the examiner has no formal framework for assessing the performance of students. Because of these limitations, the Objective Structured Clinical Examination (OSCE) and the Objective

Structured Long Examination Record (OSLER) have been developed
by medical educators. The implementation of these newer assessment processes, as part of the curriculum changes in Manchester,
will be continued because it is seen as one mechanism by which
subjective judgements in clinical examinations can be reduced. As
part of the introduction of OSCE and OSLER, examiners will be
trained in assessment techniques, and issues about ethnicity and
gender will be included in the training programme of all examiners.
The training will ultimately be made compulsory before an examiner
will be allowed to examine medical students.

At present, because of the structure of most medical schools,
there is a much greater emphasis placed on research than there is on
undergraduate and posgraduate medical education. Although the
NHS pays substantial sums of money for teaching to hospitals, most
of this money is presently concentrated in the academic university
teaching hospitals. A significant proportion of examiners come from
district general hospitals (DGH), who receive very little in return for
the effort they make. Formal training in examination techniques
would therefore not only be needed for NHS/DGH consultants but
also for those in academic institutions who are responsible for the
undergraduate educational process.

Almost all patients used in clinical exams in Manchester were
white and this could inadvertently introduce bias in the clinical
examination. Attempts will also be made to recruit more ethnic
minority patients for clinical examinations, both to reflect the reality
of the workload that future doctors will face and to ensure that all
students get a more broad-based exposure to patients from different
backgrounds. Ethnicity and gender monitoring of the results of
OSCE and OSLER examinations will become routine.

Although these measures will not in themselves eliminate the
possibility of racial bias, they may reduce it. The policy of continual
monitoring of the results of examination will enable the Manchester
examiners to assess the impact of changes that they are introducing
and take further corrective action if required.

It is unlikely that the findings that Manchester made public were
unique. It is also unlikely that the problem is confined solely to
medicine. We believe that no other medical school has analysed its
examination results in the systematic manner which was carried out
in the Faculty of Medicine. The extent of the problem that
Manchester has identified is therefore difficult to quantify. Almost
every academic discipline where the examination process involves

face to face contact between student and examiner is likely to be subject to the same biases.

The relatively simple quantitative analysis that was carried out in Manchester shows that such methods could be more widely used. Anecdote is not a satisfactory means of investigating this problem; ethnic and gender monitoring should become routine and examination results should be analysed and published using ethnicity and gender as a variable. Unless ethnic minority students can be reassured that they have the same chances of success as their white colleagues there will always be an undercurrent of thinking which believes that discrimination is a problem. In the long term this will have a detrimental impact on the institution and cause considerable resentment among an important minority of students and staff.

The openness of the institution at Manchester in highlighting the problem and setting in process a mechanism for reducing future bias should also be an example for how institutions can deal with such problems. It is not only ethnic minority students who will benefit from the reforms being instituted in Manchester, as any improvement in the methods of assessment will encourage and motivate all students equally. Manchester medical students will benefit from the outcome because the process of examination will become more transparent. In the longer term, the requirement that examiners will need to be trained and be aware of how ethnicity and gender may influence examination results will actually improve the standard and objectivity of examinations which will benefit all students. Perhaps the only note of disquiet will be from some consultants and academic staff who will need to undergo formal training in assessment techniques before they will be allowed to examine in future.

Chapter 11

Race Equality Staffing Policies in Higher Education

Gurharpal Singh

Despite the increasing focus on equal opportunities in higher education, the issue of racial equality and of ethnic minority staffing has received relatively little attention. Over the last decade, as the number of ethnic minority students has increased, the higher education system has also witnessed a considerable expansion, particularly with the end of the binary divide between the older universities and the former polytechnics (the 'new' universities). This expansion, however, and the needs of ethnic minority students, are rarely linked in terms of appropriate staffing or the status of ethnic minority academics. Indeed academics and university managers who have traditionally been reluctant to admit racial inequality in hiring or managing staff have generally relied on the pursuit of academic excellence as a counter to accusations of favouritism. In recent years, however, this defence has been effectively challenged by those seeking to improve the gender imbalance in the faculty staff of older as well as the new universities. Because this campaign has been so successful, it provides important lessons for tackling racial inequality that have so far remained relatively neglected.

This chapter will argue that there is growing evidence of racial discrimination against ethnic minority academic staff. Such discrimination needs to be seen against the background of the relative status of ethnic minority staff and the policies pursued by institutions of higher education to promote better racial equality. The effectiveness of these policies has been undermined by the lack of appropriate implementation and the quasi-privatisation of the higher education sector. In order to overcome these difficulties, a new perspective is required that includes better regulatory mechanisms and more legal and informal support for ethnic minority staff.

Discrimination against ethnic minority staff in higher education is now increasingly coming into the public domain. Although there is no systematic evidence – gathering such evidence is in itself part of the problem – of this discrimination, individual cases highlight a growing problem which the higher education sector is failing to address. For example, in a recent tribunal decision the University of Manchester was found guilty of racial discrimination against a law lecturer. The tribunal found that the university was 'negative, inadequate, even hostile'. The details of this case are worth quoting at length:

> Dr Qureshi, 41, claimed that on several occasions he had been overlooked for senior lectureships because the decision-making process at the university was racially biased. He claimed that he had been victimised because of the legal proceedings he was bringing against the university. The... tribunal found that the university had unlawfully discriminated against Dr Qureshi in his attempts to gain promotion in 1992, 1993 and 1994. It also found that the university and the second respondent, professor of law Rodney Brazier, discriminated against him and victimised him when refusing an application for study leave. (*The Times Higher Education Supplement,* 4 July 1997

Two years before, in another case which was remarkably similar, the London Guildhall University was found guilty of discrimination and victimisation towards another law lecturer. The report of this case stated:

> Dr Amir Majid, who is of Pakistani origin, is employed as a Senior Lecturer at the London Guildhall University. In 1991 he brought industrial tribunal proceedings against his employer alleging that his failure to be promoted to a principal lectureship was on grounds of race. This issue was settled with the university accepting that Dr Majid was a good candidate for appointment to principal lecturer. Later that year, however, his application for a principal lecturer post, a post which had been created to give effect to the terms of the settlement, was turned down. When another application was rejected in July 1992, Dr Majid claimed that he had been victimised for having brought the earlier proceedings. While this action was pending he claimed that he had been further victimised. In particular, his head of department had placed him last in a list of 18 recommended candidates for performance-related pay, giving him little or no chance of receiving such payment as only a limited number of awards were to be made.
>
> The industrial tribunal held that Dr Majid had been discriminated against by way of victimisation for bringing the original tribunal proceedings... Following the tribunal's decision the university agreed to

pay £15,000 for hurt feeling. (*Equal Opportunities Review*, 1995.)[1]

These two cases are interesting not only because they have come into the public sphere but also for highlighting the fact that when issues of racial discrimination are pursued by staff they become open to pressures of intimidation and victimisation, even though legislation specifically protects the complainant against victimisation. Anecdotal evidence suggests that there is considerable dog-fighting over racial inequality by ethnic minority staff, but these bitter struggles rarely come to the fore (*The Guardian*, 7 May 1996). One reason for this lack of openness is that in a public imag-conscious environment universities have become adept at managing public and legal exposure, even to the point of including confidentiality clauses in pre-tribunal settlements. At the same time university staff are reluctant to challenge such pressure because of fear, intimidation, victimisation and the lack of mobility within the profession. When to these factors is added the considerable weight of professional stigmatisation associated with any claims of racial inequality, the sense of hopelessness can become overwhelming.[2]

RACE EQUALITY AND THE REPRESENTATION OF ETHNIC MINORITY STAFF IN HIGHER EDUCATION

In order to establish the broader context within which issues of race equality within higher education can be assessed, we need to know something about the sector and the representation of ethnic minority staff within it. The higher education sector includes the traditional universities, the new universities and colleges of higher education and other recognised institutions with degree-awarding powers. These institutions receive most of their funding from the Higher Education Funding Council for England (HEFCE). Similar institutions in Wales and Scotland are supported by their own funding councils. These councils provide support for teaching and research. The majority of academic staff employed in universities are engaged

---

1   There were many other interesting aspects to this case which are not provided in the brief summary. For a more detailed summary see *Equal Opportunities Review* No. 25, Autumn 1995.

2   It is interesting to note that whereas the advocates of better gender equality in academia are rarely seen as intellectually underdeveloped, the racialisation of ethnic categories has created a situation where ethnic minority staff are reluctant to deploy the same tactics for fear of (white) professional stigmatisation.

in either or both of these tasks. However, universities and colleges of higher education are also large bureaucracies, and a substantial degree of administration is a regular part of staff workload as well as being the main preoccupation of senior staff who manage the institutions. Over the last two decades, as the unit of resource has declined, the universities and colleges have emulated business methods to retain and expand student recruitment, encourage commercial research and sponsorship, undertake market-oriented curriculum development, and develop better systems of management and control.

Concerns about the ability of higher education institutions to implement effective race equality policies therefore extend beyond mere recruitment. There are, I believe, profound misgivings also about promotions – as highlighted in the above cases – access to research funding, curriculum development and appropriate provision for staff development with particular access to administrative experience – an area regularly identified as a necessary requirement for promotions to the higher levels. These are essential dimensions of professional development, and if there is discrimination or in-equality in their administration, the consequences, as has been illustrated, can be devastating.

Viewed in a comparative context – other sectors of state and local employment, e.g., health, primary and secondary education, social service – it is reasonable to assume that in terms of the development of race equality policies the higher education sector is no exception.

Statistics provided by the Higher Education Statistical Agency (HESA) suggest that the representation of ethnic minority staff is broadly in line with their proportion of the total population in the UK (Table 11.1). These statistics are based on a 56.3 per cent ethnicity identification rate for 88,160 UK nationality and 26,561 non-UK nationality staff (HESA, 1996). What is striking about these figures is that, given the background of the ethnic minorities from the New Commonwealth countries and their length of settlement in the UK, the proportion of ethnic minority staff of total is relatively stable. As some ethnic minority groups are now tending to excel in education – witness the high percentage of ethnic minority students – the issue perhaps should be of *over* rather than *proportionate* or *under*-representation. Clearly within the different ethnic minorities there are variations, though perhaps they are not too significant as only the 'Other' category manages to obtain a representation of more than 1 per cent. The main variation in the representation of ethnic minority staff, however, comes in terms of citizenship status. If non-UK

nationals are considered, the overall picture is much more plural,
with those of Chinese ethnic background representing 7.61 per cent
of all staff. In fact in all the ethnic minority categories identified, the
representation of non-UK nationals is greater than that of UK
nationals. This important difference may be explained by the need to
hire staff of outstanding international achievement; equally, as we
shall see below, it may reflect a particular structural position within
the higher education sector which is obscured by the aggregate data.

**Table 11.1   Ethnic background of academic staff in institutions of
higher education 1994–95**

column percentages

Ethnicity	UK nationality	Non-UK nationality
White	96.42	75.42
Black Caribbean	0.26	0.75
Black African	0.19	2.46
Black Other	0.12	0.38
Indian	0.81	3.64
Pakistani	0.21	0.53
Bangladeshi	0.04	0.23
Chinese	0.34	7.61
Asian Other	0.44	3.61
Other	1.13	5.32
Total	100.0	100.0

Source: HESA, 1996

There is some evidence to suggest that although the representation
of ethnic minority staff, especially of non-UK national background,
appears healthy, their status by employment function is relatively
unfavourable compared to white staff. If it is assumed that the
category of full-time teaching and research represents the most
desirable status, the position of ethnic minority staff is slightly worse
than the representation depicted in Table 11.1. A large number of
non-UK nationality staff, for example, appear to be employed for
research -only purposes. The high aggregate figure for staff of non-
UK nationality of Chinese ethnic background in Table 11.1 is
reflected in the same ethnic group occupying 15.6 per cent of
research-only posts among the total non-UK nationality staff (see
Table 11.2). Likewise, non-UK national Indians and Black Africans
hold 4.13 and 2.28 per cent of the research-only posts respectively.
Although more data are required to identify the specific functions of

academics, given that most research staff are on fixed term contracts, it is probably valid to surmise that non-UK staff are disportionately employed on non-tenure research contracts.

Table 11.2   Ethnic background of academic staff according to employment function 1994–95

UK nationality

Ethnicity	Full-time			Part-time		
	Teaching only	Research only	Teaching & research	Teaching only	Research only	Teaching & research
White	97.70	94.50	96.91	97.60	97.32	96.46
Black Caribbean	0.37	0.26	0.24	0.19	0.13	0.21
Black African	0.21	0.27	0.16	0.06	0.13	0.21
Black Other	0.19	0.17	0.09	0.06	0.27	0.15
Indian	0.73	1.73	0.67	0.65	0.68	0.68
Pakistani	0.07	0.46	0.18	0.00	0.13	0.12
Bangladeshi	0.05	0.06	0.03	0.00	0.06	0.03
Chinese	0.13	0.78	0.24	0.06	0.20	0.18
Asian Other	0.43	0.71	0.36	0.32	0.61	0.37
Other	0.98	1.32	1.09	0.92	1.64	1.53

Non-UK nationality

Ethnicity	Full-time			Part-time		
	Teaching only	Research only	Teaching & research	Teaching only	Research only	Teaching & research
White	79.69	64.86	81.41	87.44	79.42	88.52
Black Caribbean	1.36	0.28	0.96	0.00	0.00	0.77
Black African	3.07	2.28	2.51	1.39	2.28	1.24
Black Other	0.85	0.23	0.42	0.00	0.28	0.77
Indian	3.58	4.13	3.35	1.86	3.71	1.86
Pakistani	0.51	0.80	0.36	0.46	1.14	0.31
Bangladeshi	0.17	0.52	0.07	0.00	0.57	0.00
Chinese	2.38	15.61	3.28	2.79	4.00	1.24
Asian Other	3.92	5.23	2.60	2.79	2.57	1.39
Other	4.49	6.01	4.99	3.25	6.00	3.87

Source: HESA, 1996

Third in terms of part-time teaching, ethnic minorities of UK nationality are under-represented in the three functions identified – teaching only, research only, and teaching and research. In contrast, ethnic minorities of non-UK nationality compare favourably with those of UK nationality. This figure is surprising given the diffi-culties associated with obtaining employment clearance for academic staff. These figures probably conceal a large number of PhD students who are close to having completed their dissertations, because otherwise the recruitment of such staff would not be cost effective.

Overall, while the figures are too incomplete to make firm generalisations, the following inferences appear justified. The position of the ethnic minority academic staff seems to be structurally marginal with many confined to specific roles such as teaching or research. Second, proportionately more ethnic minority staff of non-UK national background appear to be on research-only contracts than UK nationals.

Trade unions working within the higher education sector have recognised that there is something profoundly wrong. To some extent they have been spurred into action by the increasing requirement to keep data on the ethnic background of students and staff. In 1996 the Association of University Teachers' survey of 8,500 members showed that only 0.3 per cent of these were African or Afro-Caribbean (*The Guardian,* 7 May 1996) whereas 14 per cent of the students were from the ethnic minorities (HEFCE, 1996a). In 1996 the National Association of Teachers in Further and Higher Education (NATFHE) produced *Race Equality in Further and Higher Education* drawing on the practical advice given to further education sector managers on equality of opportunity by the Commission for Racial Equality (CRE) and the Equal Opportunities Commission (EOC). But these developments, almost 20 years after the creation of the CRE, are perhaps indicative of the inertia within institutions of higher education and the delayed response of the trade unions in dealing with the matter.

THE DEVELOPMENT OF RACE EQUALITY POLICIES
IN HIGHER EDUCATION

Most institutions of higher education have been slow to respond in developing effective policies of race equality. A survey conducted in 1994 found that while 73 per cent of the responding institutions kept a statistical record of the gender of their staff, the figure fell to 52 per cent for ethnicity, and only 37 per cent had adopted action plans to implement equal opportunities policies (CUCO, 1994). Given the generic context within which equal opportunities policies are often implemented, it may be safe to assume that race equality as an issue for higher education managers is probably very low down the order of priorities. To evaluate how the higher education sector has responded to race equality, it is appropriate to contrast the higher education experience with the ideal models of effective race equality policy implementation.

In the 1980s researchers working within the area of race equality and the local state identified three strands in such policies. First, these included promotional policies which suggested an awareness of the issue. Typically this implied a declaration as an equal opportunities employer, a need to increase staff and external awareness of the issue, and to undertake staff training. Second, there was the emphasis on the equality of treatment in terms of service delivery. All aspects of institutional practice were critically evaluated with reference to providing services to clients with a view to identifying structures, practices and policies that may have constituted unfair treatment. Finally, the issue of the recruitment, status and promotion of ethnic minority staff was evaluated by setting up ethnic monitoring, identifying patterns of (under-)recruitment, and establishing future targets. The link with recruitment and the other two aspects was essential:

> Racially discriminatory outcomes were not solely the function of organisational procedures but also related to the under-representation or exclusion of black and ethnic minority staff. (Solomos and Singh, 1990)

An effective policy combined all three elements supported by rigorous monitoring and a political determination to achieve policy goals.

With reference to these three strands, how have the universities and colleges performed? Probably because promotional policies are least cost-effective and onerous to implement, these have been taken up most. A typical search through the *The Times Higher Educational Supplement* or *The Guardian Higher* reveals a fulsome reference to equal opportunities with the frequent comment that the institution is 'an equal opportunities employer'. Some institutions which are probably aware that this commitment might be difficult to demonstrate have added riders such as 'working towards equal opportunities'. Despite this qualification, a study done in 1991 of university prospectuses found that out of 53 only 4 were judged to 'contain explicit statements about equal opportunities' (Jewson et al, 1991: 186). Indeed in the overall representation of ethnic minorities in university prospectuses it was suggested that:

> the visual multi-ethnic presence in university prospectuses seems to reflect a wish to attract lucrative overseas markets, rather than a conscious effort to reflect a multi-cultural Britain. (Jewson et al, 1991)

The same study made an interesting observation on the role of staff:

> As far as staffing is concerned, the visual image conveyed by the prospectuses is one suggesting that ethnic minority academic staff are under-represented. Only 14 of the 53 prospectuses showed any such staff, while only four showed ethnic minority academic-related staff and none showed ethnic minority support staff. (Jewson et al, 1991)

Symbolic promotional policies have also been accompanied by half-hearted measures to evaluate aspects of service delivery. In some cases universities have been compelled to undertake this revision under the threat of legal action. The CRE's investigation into recruitment procedures at St George's Medical School in 1988, for example, exposed systematic discrimination against ethnic minorities and women (Williams et al, 1989). Against the background of raising ethnic minority students, it is important that all aspects of student experience – examination performance, student services, drop-out rates, the curriculum, careers advice, industrial placement – are thoroughly examined to evaluate possible patterns of discrimination. To date there is little evidence that these dimensions have been critically reviewed. Indeed, in spite of evidence that students from ethnic minorities tend to fail courses more frequently than non-ethnic minority students (Singh, 1990; van Dyke, and Esmail Chapters 9 and 10 in this book), or are regularly disadvantaged in work placements, there is a marked reluctance by the universities to address these questions. In cases where staff have often raised issues of student experience, it is not uncommon to find stereotypical responses or suggestions that student recruitment is the key issue to overcoming entrenched prejudice and bias.[3]

Recently, market pressures – declining student recruitment – have compelled higher education institutions to re-examine the curriculum. Often professional courses – health, education and social work – have been adapted to ethnic minority student needs. Similar modifications have also been attempted in the humanities and the social sciences with degree programmes in South Asian studies, Caribbean studies and cultural and religious studies with reference to migrants of New Commonwealth decent. Even these initiatives, however, are piecemeal, marginal and generally predicated on local ethnic minority groups funding or supporting such curricular development. One of the ironies of the growing marketisation of

---

3   This observation is drawn from interviews carried out for this research with ethnic minority staff. For obvious reasons they remain anonymous.

university courses is that, whereas greater emphasis is being placed on increasing ethnic minority access to higher education, the reality of such rhetoric, especially in the new universities, is that they see ethnic communities as a resource, providing the main funding for such courses, either through conventional resources that were targeted for ethnic minorities (inner-city, EU aid) or private endowments. University managers may have seen the resource potential of the 'access' issue but they have lacked the vision to attract ethnic minority students through the better development of the curriculum for ethnic minority students – which in fact could also enhance the recruitment of overseas students through related area studies programmes.

Since most of the focus of development of race equality policies has remained at the promotional or service delivery level, concerns about staffing and its relationship with the other two aspects have not, paradoxically, been at the forefront. The emphasis on individual academic achievement has enabled managers of the higher education sector to propound an ideology of colour-blindness. However, as evidence of discrimination increases and statistical monitoring begins to reveal the structural location of ethnic minority staff, it seems that institutions will have to face a broad range of issues concerning recruitment, promotion, under-representation at the higher levels and the general marginality of ethnic minority staff. There are some indications that as a result of these developments, the first hesitant steps have begun to be taken to establish monitoring processes. At present these processes are very crude, focus only on initial recruitment and exclude promotions, allocations of internal research grants, development projects, study leave and administrative experience. Establishing comprehensive monitoring and evaluation of these elements will certainly enable managerial discretion to be better evaluated but, given the general reluctance to develop race equality policies, it seems unlikely that universities and colleges will necessarily take these further steps.

In contrast to the experience of local authorities in areas of high ethnic minority populations in the 1980s, the institutions of higher education have failed to develop integrated policies for promoting racial equality and have not recognised the link between promotional policies and service delivery on the one hand and appropriate academic staffing on the other. As staffing was the key element in changing the colour-blind culture of many of the local authorities, the relatively low priority given to it suggests that the groundswell of concern by ethnic minority academic staff about racial inequality in higher education is unlikely to provide the momentum of rapid organisational change.

PROSPECTS FOR CHANGE

Apart from the general reluctance to embrace the full implication of race equality policies, there are other reasons to believe that for most institutions of higher education, racial equality will be a low priority in the medium term.

First, financial considerations, together with changing thinking about effective race equality, have increasingly promoted the merger of all aspects of inequality into a single agenda for the promotion of equality. To some extent this process was evident in the demise of race equality units in local authorities and the merging of their work with other units working on gender, disability, and sexual orientation. Institutions of higher education never had sufficient resources or inclination to treat these dimensions separately. But by merging them in the pursuit of one central objective of equality there are dangers that differences in inequality will tend to be overlooked. Thus the powerful lobby that supports greater gender equality within academia is able to obtain greater responsiveness from institutions of higher education, even though in some cases the representation of women within the higher grades is substantially greater than that of ethnic minorities, leading to thinly concealed affirmative action policies. There are, in short, many qualitative differences in the pursuit of gender and racial equality.

Second, the growing privatisation of the higher education sector – the emphasis on external income generation, student tuition fees, declining source of income from the state – is likely to reduce the element of public control and the ability to influence the policy of higher education institutions. This process was evident in the creation of the new universities, which became uncoupled from local authority control at the end of the 1980s. Interestingly prior to this development many local authorities had developed action plans for policy change but these were put on hold as the new institutions demonstrated their autonomy and new-found status as universities. Further moves towards market-driven higher education will certainly reduce the effectiveness of policies designed to benefit groups – a tendency also likely to be reinforced by the increasing patterns of global academic recruitment which may depress the recruitment of ethnic minorities of UK nationality while increasing the proportion of non-UK nationality ethnic minorities because of salary costs.

Third, the recent Dearing Committee report on higher education has reaffirmed the conventional wisdom that the issue of equality in the sector is simply one of student recruitment and human resources. Indeed, the committee recommended that:

> ...all institutions should, as part of their human resources policy, maintain equal opportunities policies, and, over the medium term, should identify and remove barriers which inhibit recruitment and progression for particular groups and monitor and publish their progress towards greater equality for all groups. (*The Times Higher Education Supplement,* 25 July 1997)

The use of the word 'maintain' is indicative, implying that equal opportunities are in place and perhaps effective in their operation (cf. Modood and Shiner, 1994). The suggestion that student recruitment and progression from particular groups may be disadvantaged appears to contradict the effectiveness of existing policies. By proposing that this is an issue for the medium term, the committee has both overlooked the significance of the subject within the sector and given unclear guidance for the development of effective policies prior to fulfilment of the requirement to increase wider participation from all social and ethnic backgrounds. In light of the previous experience, it is reasonable to assume that most institutions will view the Dearing recommendations as affirmation of existing institutional policies.

Yet despite these formidable obstacles a number of steps can be taken which could radically alter the position and address some of the issues of racial inequality that are being identified. Essentially they are fourfold:

1 strengthen the regulatory mechanism of central institutions;
2 encourage institutions to disaggregate aspects of inequality;
3 give greater rights to individuals to pursue action against institutions;
4 establish informal networks of ethnic minority staff who, working with or without the trade unions, could provide support and guidance for individuals with such grievances.

Most privatisations, especially of former national utilities, have been accompanied by the establishment of regulatory frameworks. Something similar has happened with the formation of HEFCE and the Quality Assurance Agency. These bodies have considerable powers to monitor the work of universities and colleges. HEFCE, for example, is responsible for the funding for these institutions and the monitoring of teaching and research. Whereas the assessment of teaching undertaken by HEFCE visits takes full account of student experience, there is no provision in the assessment framework for linking this with staffing (HEFCE, 1996b). This contrasts sharply with the Office for Standards in Education (OFSTED) framework for the inspection of schools where the issue of equal opportunities is explicitly identified with appropriate teaching role models (OFSTED, 1995). Furthermore, because the framework of assessment in higher education institutions seeks to evaluate provision in terms of the providers' own self-assessment, there is considerable room for manoeuvre over difficult issues. Similarly, despite the 1996 Research Assessment Exercise, issues of equal opportunities and racial equality were largely ignored, with profound consequences for the assessment of particular subjects and individuals. Given the new regulatory role envisaged for HEFCE and the Quality Assurance Agency in light of the Dearing proposals, it is certainly possible to develop more explicit controls to eradicate discrimination. One suggestion put forward by a victim of racial discrimination is for the HEFCE to copy the model of the Research Assessment Exercise and to link teaching and research funding to league tables of higher education institutions' equal opportunities policies (Dr Asif Qureshi, quoted in *The Times Higher Education Supplement,* 26 September 1997).

Second, where institutions produce monitoring data and this is available to individuals and trade unions, it is important that pressure is exerted for the disaggregation of the data in terms of the different categories – ethnicity, gender, disability etc – as well as by employment status. All too often institutions are keen to demonstrate their commitment by presenting data that are not meaningful or in a way that puts the best gloss on it. A critical reading of such data can become an effective tool forcing reluctant institutions to undertake further monitoring.

Third, there is a need to further strengthen the legal framework to enable individuals to undertake legal action. The success rate for cases taken under the Race Relations Act (1976) is very low. In 1991, according to Department of Employment figures, only 13 per cent of the discrimination cases were successful, and it is extremely difficult to prove discrimination in most cases, especially indirect discrimination (NATFHE, 1996). Although the lifting of the ceiling in compensation to successful complainants in 1995 should act as a deterrent to potential defendants not to discriminate, it is unlikely to function as a sufficient threat. There is much discussion currently about strengthening legislation to curtail inequality. If any such proposals are made, they certainly need to examine the difficulties often encountered by academic staff in accumulating and getting the appropriate evidence. It is interesting to note that the two successful cases cited at the beginning were brought by law lecturers.

Finally, perhaps the most effective mechanism for short-term change is the establishment of a support network of ethnic minority staff. Some trade unions, like NATFHE, have a black sections group, but because staff are often reluctant to formally approach the trade unions, an alternative voluntary network could provide a valuable resource for sharing experiences, information, details of comparable cases and evidence of good practice. Again to draw the contrast with the local authority experience of the 1980s, often the informal 'black worker groups' had the most impact in terms of monitoring the effectiveness of race and equal opportunities programmes.

CONCLUSION

It is no longer viable for universities and colleges of higher education to argue that they are immune from the problems of racial inequality in the management of their affairs. The growing evidence to the contrary suggests that the issue needs urgent consideration. There is a widespread perception among ethnic minority academic staff that there is a virtual 'glass ceiling' in the senior and executive positions; and in the lower levels there is considerable discrimination, disadvantage and over-representation in particular areas, such as research-only posts. Some ethnic minority staff, as we have seen, are no longer prepared to suffer in silence and, at considerable risks to their own professional development, are prepared to speak out. This may produce a snowballing effect where the issue becomes serious enough to produce positive outcomes. Past experience, however, suggests that such optimism might be unjustified. But if Dearing's vision of a lifelong learning society with wider access to higher education is to be realised, racial inequality must not be allowed to act as a permanent exclusionary barrier to the progress of staff and the students.[4]

---

4   A new research project on ethnic minority staff is taking place in 1998. For details please contact Joe Charlesworth at the Commission for Racial Equality or Tariq Modood, an editor of this volume.

Chapter 12

Conclusion

Tariq Modood and Tony Acland

Research which has race and higher education as its focus has grown considerably in recent years, and has broadened in range. The research and discussion reported in this volume are representative of the main kinds of quantitative and qualitative analysis being conducted in England and Wales during the 1990s. This chapter draws upon the main conclusions of these works in order to review the position and the experiences of ethnic minorities in higher education. The second half of the chapter focuses upon the key policy issues and dilemmas which confront policy makers and outlines a strategy for improving the experience of ethnic minorities in higher education.

RACE IN HIGHER EDUCATION

Until 1990, the main debate concerning ethnic minorities and higher education centred upon an unsubstantiated impression that ethnic minorities were under-represented in higher education. Systematic data collection was instituted in the 1990s and it soon became clear that ethnic minorities, as a whole, are more successful in achieving university entry than white applicants (Taylor, 1992; Modood, 1993). The analysis offered by Modood in Chapter 3 of this book suggests that over-representation is the norm for almost all ethnic minority groups compared to white groups.

This is not to say that there is no issue of ethnic minority under-representation in higher education. Whilst showing greater overall representation for ethnic minorities, the above studies reveal that gender differences exist, with Caribbean men and Bangladeshi women most likely to be under-represented. Caribbean entrants are also disproportionately mature students and probably part time. Moreover, equivalent qualified Caribbean and Pakistani applicants may be less likely to be offered a place than other groups (Modood and Shiner, 1994). The situation therefore is uneven across groups. Moreover, some, probably most, minority groups (though not all) are more likely to be found in less prestigious institutions.

The reason why researchers were slow to recognise the importance of higher education was not simply because of the limitations in the quantitative data that were available. Qualitative researchers and theorists too were slow to pick up what was happening. Gillborn's review of qualitative work in schools in Chapter 2 gives a good account of some of the progress made in ethnographic research into race in schools. For example, the understanding of racism was extended beyond overtly expressed prejudice and discrimination to include perceptions of groups implicit in what is said and done. Moreover, there was a recognition that racist assumptions about groups increasingly drew upon the perceived culture of groups for their explanatory power (cultural racism) rather than biology (Modood, 1997). This made it easier to see that different groups of people were quite differently stereotyped and treated; Asians and Caribbeans were subject to different as well as similar forms of racism, and this varied by gender as well. What is striking, however, is that this research was not alert to the high levels of motivation and determination among ethnic minority pupils which the qualification levels and entry into higher education have now substantiated and which, as we have seen in this book, qualitative research in higher education is revealing.

Qualitative schools research has become alive to ethnic minority agency, on how subordinate or marginal groups are not just passive but contribute to the shaping of situations, whether this be in schools or other social contexts. But largely because this research was structured by questions about racism, the main agency it was able to identify was resistance to racism (Modood, 1990). Hence while this research was able to demonstrate that ethnicity was real in schools and shapes educational opportunities, it was confined to ethnicity only as it related directly to racism. This no doubt is linked to another limitation of this body of research. Ethnographers seem to be able to focus on Caribbean female agency (Fuller, 1980; Mac an Ghaill, 1988; Mirza, 1992) and Caribbean male agency (Mac an Ghaill, 1988; Gillborn, 1990; Sewell,1997) but Asian agency seems to be marginal to these accounts. The irony is that in the period of time in which some South Asian groups were academically distinguishing themselves, ethnographic schools research was mainly concept-

ualising them as victims (for an ethnographic study that is sensitive
to Asian female agency, see Basit 1997).

With an empirical focus on Caribbean women, Mirza has
challenged the assumption that racial agency in schools or elsewhere
must be seen in terms of 'resistance' to racism (Mirza, 1992). As she
argues in Chapter 4, the concept of anti-racist resistance offers a
one-dimensionsal model of what it is to be black, and, in particular,
robs black people of the complexity and depth of their lived
experience by defining them in terms of the 'other'. This particularly
marginalises women as it deploys a masculinist and confrontational
model of radical social change. Mirza suggests that just because
Caribbean women exhibit scholastic success and seek rewarding
careers, it does not mean that they are less concerned with black
dignity and community welfare than men. Indeed, their commitment
to 'raising the race', which is so clearly evident in the unpaid
parenting and community work that they do, may be part of the
motivation that drives their academic and employment goals. It is
perhaps worth remarking that this interconnectedness between
personal/family, academic and economic success with community
pride and community service may seem to manifest itself more easily
among Caribbean women than men, but it seems to be applicable in
equal measure to South Asian men and women.

While the orientation of most research on race and education to
date has been in seeking explanations of why minorities are not
doing as well as their white peers, it has not engaged with questions
that could explain why some ethnic minority groups – not just as
individuals but as *groups* – might do better than their white peers. It
is clear, therefore, that we need more, not less, research which
focuses upon variations within university application and admission
patterns. We need to know considerably more about the way in
which, for example, applicants from Bangladeshi and Pakistani
backgrounds fare worse than those of Indian origin.[1] Ethnic differences in application and entry statistics are further complicated by
residential location and the continuing divide between 'old' and 'new'
universities, with ethnic minorities achieving higher admission rates
in the latter institutions. Class too is a factor, with applications more
likely in all ethnic groups to come from middle class backgrounds,
though South Asians from working-class backgrounds are more

---

1   Tariq Modood and Michael Shiner are currently undertaking a study to
examine the possible influence of A-level projected grades by teachers on
UCAS application forms on differential rates of university entry. Further
details can be obtained from Tariq Modood.

likely to apply to and enter higher education than the working classes as a whole. Indeed, despite all the difficulties associated with migration, cultural and linguistic adaptation, racism and a disadvantaged parental occupational profile, most minority groups are producing greater proportions of applications and admissions to higher education than the white population. It is important that further research combines qualitative and quantitative research in order to tell us more about these complex application and admission patterns.

REASONS FOR HIGHER APPLICATION RATES BY ETHNIC MINORITIES

The large presence of ethnic minorities in higher education has made it possible to study the reasons for the increased representation of ethnic students in higher education. Several such studies are represented in this book. This research, though based on limited samples and locations, suggests that almost all students from ethnic minority backgrounds were highly motivated and determined to enter higher education. Male and female individuals received a great deal of encouragement from their families – people, of course, who came to Britain to improve their own and especially their children's socio-economic lot. Many families, in particular those of South Asian origin, valued education as an important goal, in itself, as well as a means for obtaining a successful career. According to the Heist survey (Chapter 5), a much greater proportion of ethnic minority families valued education highly compared to white families. So strong was parental pressure that, for some, they were left with no other choice than to enter higher education. In any case, most ethnic minority students shared their parents' values, with education seen as a means to improve family status as well as their financial situation. Many considered achievement in higher education as the most effective way of combating racism in the employment market.

High motivation levels were found less among Caribbean males, compared to females from the same group and African males (Chapters 5 and 6). Caribbean students themselves felt that the main reason for this difference was the very high level of racism and sense of social rejection experienced by Caribbean males compared to Caribbean females and other ethnic minorities. Also important was the perception that Caribbean males were not subjected to the tight family control of females in their households, who were driven to conform and study. These factors combined to limit Caribbean male interest in higher education as a means to achieve status and material goals. Feeling rejected and harassed by white society, Caribbean males had the freedom from family control to develop alternative means of obtaining material and status objectives.

When applying to university or college, many ethnic minorities considered carefully what kind of institutions they wished to study in. Research findings (Chapters 5 and 6) suggest that ethnic minority students, particularly Asian women, were more likely to choose local higher education institutions (particularly new universities) than white students. To a lesser extent, ethnic minority students were attracted to institutions which had a significant number of students from their own ethnic group.

LEARNING EXPERIENCE AND ACHIEVEMENT PATTERNS IN HIGHER EDUCATION

New research has sought to examine the actual learning experiences and achievement patterns of ethnic minority students in higher education institutions. This new focus is an important development because, as earlier research into schools has shown, experiences of racism and of inappropriate institutional support can prejudice students' learning experiences, reduce their levels of success and career options and even lower their career expectations.

There have been two major types of research in higher education institutions which have focused upon the experiences of ethnic minorities in higher education institutions. Examples of both types of research have been included in this volume. Research reported by van Dyke (Chapter 9) and Esmail and Dewart (Chapter 10) investigated ethnic students' retention, progression and achievement rates. Other research (Chapters 6, 7 and 8) analysed qualitative evidence of ethnic students' perceptions and experiences in particular higher education institutions.

Unfortunately, reliable national data for either kind of analysis do not exist and we are currently dependent upon case studies of particular institutions to provide us with a picture of the learning experiences and achievements of ethnic minority students in higher education. With such a gap in our knowledge of the national picture, it is important to exercise some caution when drawing conclusions from case study research.

Nevertheless, research is being done on student achievement rates with interesting results. The two studies included in this book look at what could be regarded as very different levels in the hierarchy of academic institutions. Van Dyke's case study (Chapter 9) is based on two new universities, two of a large range of polytechnics that were made universities in 1992. Located in London, they have among the highest proportions of ethnic minorities of any institutions, with many mature students and many studying part-time. Her analysis focuses on four courses, a social science degree, two business degrees and an electrical engineering degree, and looks at differences in retention, progression and achievement rates among ethnic minorities. She found that Caribbean students fared appreciably worse than other groups, though they performed better in course work than in exams. In contrast, South Asian students performed particularly well compared to all other groups, including white students. Whilst noting the high levels of motivation, confidence and commitment of Asian students, van Dyke suggested that a range of measures were needed to combat the relatively low achievement record of Caribbean students.

The other case study (Chapter 10) is at the other end of the academic hierarchy, where only those with the highest A-level grades are accepted, namely a medical degree course. It is a course where Asians, primarily Indians, are well represented, with 30 per cent of men and nearly 20 per cent of women having non-European names. Yet despite the highly academic environment, Esmail and Dewart identified clear evidence of inequality in final medical examinations. They found that, whilst Asian students generally performed better than other groups in anonymous written examinations, the predominantly white consultants tended to fail Asians in the practical interpersonal assessments in hospital situations. This case study was particularly interesting because, as an action-based research project, discussion of the study findings led to the institution developing effective strategies to reduce the possibility of racial discrimination in the assessment process. New measures adopted included the expanded use of anonymous marking and the introduction of new objective criteria-based assessment, backed up by training for assessors.

It is worth noting that the conclusions of these two studies point in different directions. While both suggest that Asians are likely to reach a higher grade relative to whites in written objective tests, the first study suggests that some minority groups might benefit if less assessment were of a written examination sort; the second suggests that where objective marking is relaxed or is not possible, there the scope for bias will enter. Indeed, in the first study, too, students complained of being judged subjectively on style and presentation and not enough on 'the facts'. It is not therefore clear whether the racial discrimination will be lessened by more or less rigid assessment, or a particular mix of methods of assessment, or whether the solution will vary depending on the academic level and which group one is trying to assist. Clearly, a lot more work needs to be done on assessment in general and ethnic bias in particular. It should be done with sample sizes that allow for a gender breakdown and for a breakdown of the Asian category, for it is very likely that the conclusions that are emerging from composite Asian samples may turn out to be true for Indians only, not for Bangladeshis and Pakistanis, were such breakdown possible.

EXPERIENCES AND PERCEPTIONS OF
HIGHER EDUCATION INSTITUTIONS

Statistical analyses on their own can not provide a complete picture of the nature of ethnic minority experience in higher education. We also need to examine qualitative research findings which focus in depth upon the perceptions and experiences of ethnic minorities in higher education institutions. Indeed, the perceptions and experiences of ethnic minorities themselves affect the learning process, including the relationships established with tutors and the way in which students participate in group and individual exercises.

Qualitative research (Chapters 5 and 6) has noted that ethnic minority students' perceptions of higher education institutions are influenced before entry, particularly as a result of reading prospectuses and other pre-admission literature. Prospective students sometimes wished to ascertain the ethnic mix of the institution and the surrounding community. They also wished to gauge how seriously the institution viewed and responded to equal opportunity and race issues. Some students were hesitant about entering institutions with small numbers of students or staff from their own ethnic background.

Several chapters (5 to 8) demonstrated the concern of some ethnic minority students with what they considered to be an inappropriate curriculum in their institutions. Although students recognised the growth of race and ethnic studies optional units, they spoke of 'opportunities lost' for the inclusion of equal opportunity and race issues in the core curriculum. This finding was confirmed by a recent report from the Higher Education Quality Council (HEQC, 1996). Whilst recognising that many equal opportunities measures had been adopted by higher education institutions, HEQC noted that the curriculum had received very little attention. Institutions should clearly be thinking about more multicultural curricula but it should not be seen as a sop to ethnic minorities. Chapter 8, based on an extremely detailed and systematic study in an institution where ethnic minorities make up about half the student population, suggests that the demand for a more diversity based curriculum is found as much among the white students who wish to be properly prepared for life and work in a multicultural society as from ethnic minority students. Indeed, as yet, a significant minority but not a majority of the latter want a more multicultural curriculum, and some minority groups, like Africans, desire this less than their white peers.

A number of chapters in this book report how ethnic minority students were very disappointed with the relatively low numbers of ethnic minority lecturers in higher education institutions. They point out the importance of black role models and success figures to inspire and support ethnic minority students. Institutions with predominantly white tutors were viewed with suspicion. According to Paul Allen (Chapter 7), such a perception reinforced students' experience of racism in their daily lives and made them suspicious and hostile to their university. Allen argues that black students' 'scepticality' led them to depend upon black student networks in order to create 'black space' to insulate themselves from racism in higher education institutions.

The experience of racism in both learning and social situations is reported in a number of studies in this book (Chapters 6, 7, 8 and 10). Experiences reported involving tutors ranged from the inappropriate use of language to accusations of discrimination in assessments. Verbal abuse and discrimination in clubs and societies were cited as common examples of racism from white students.

A particularly difficult curriculum and assessment issue to resolve is the controversial role of work placements on academic programmes, in particular on business, engineering and applied science courses. For many years work placements have been considered essential for the development of work skills and for promoting an understanding of the interface between theory and practice. However, some ethnic minority students, particularly Caribbean males, have argued that placements provide opportunities for racial discrimination by employing agencies. Much of this criticism relates to the way in which the placement application process tends to be conducted, particularly where photographs are used. Although a follow-up investigation of placement application and selection procedures (Chapter 6) did not substantiate student fears, there remains the need to alleviate students' perception that there are opportunities for discrimination by agencies. It may not be enough to suspend the use of photographs in the placement application process, at least not for those whose names betray their non-European origins.

THE WAY FORWARD

A comprehensive strategy is needed to improve the experience of ethnic minorities in higher education. Discussion of recent research and controversies in this volume demonstrates that a number of changes in educational policy are required to build a higher education system in which ethnic minorities experience genuine equality with white students.

Strategies designed to achieve equality should address the educational needs and experiences of ethnic minority students throughout their educational career – from school to graduation, to admission to higher education and from graduation to entry into the employment (or unemployment) market. Whilst the evidence reported in this book suggests that positive measures should be taken to support all ethnic minority students, particular attention should be focused on those groups who continue to be under-represented and who experience the lowest rates of success in higher education.

The school context

Gillborn's review of school research in the last ten years (Chapter 2) has clear implications for the teaching profession. There is a need for teacher education to confront in a more effective manner the issue of racist stereotypes and classroom discourse which can lead to the, often unintentional, erosion of Caribbean and Asian students' confidence and security in multi-ethnic schools. Similarly, there is a need for a review of staff development for trainee and experienced teachers to address these problems. Moreover, if the main source of racist antagonism for Caribbean students were teachers, Asian students were subject to considerable racist harassment and bullying by other pupils (see also Wrench and Qureshi, 1996).

It is also important to confront the growing concern of exclusionary practices which disproportionately affect Caribbean pupils, and a priority for establishing effective strategies to combat racist bullying in and around the school. Whilst such matters remain unsatisfactorily addressed, the unde-representation of Caribbean males in higher education can be expected to continue. Yet, the fact of differential racism means that racial equality action has to be sensitively approached and without the assumption that all forms of racialisation can be tackled in a uniform way.

As John Bird (1992, 1996) has demonstrated in Bristol, there is a need for close liaison between higher education institutions and schools in order to raise awareness among black and ethnic minority pupils of the opportunities available in higher education. It is important for such liaison to involve ethnic minority students as mentors. Such students can provide role models, encouragement and support for young ethnic minority students to progress to higher education. Not only is it important for students to visit schools, but there need to be follow-up visits for pupils to sample life in higher education.

Pre-admission information

Like all students, ethnic minority applicants are often dependent upon prospectuses and other pre-admission literature to give them a clear picture of the suitability of the institution for their needs. It is important for institutions to review their marketing and advertising materials and processes to ensure that accurate and comprehensive information is provided to guide students' choice, including pictures and information on ethnic representation, facilities and resources in the institution and the immediate neighbourhood.

The use of open days is one way in which institutions can supplement pre-admission literature. When thoughtfully organised, with the participation of student peer guides from a range of ethnic backgrounds, open days can effectively give students a glimpse of particular institutions. Such a strategy can only be useful if peer guides are given sufficient freedom to answer questions and provide prospective students with an accurate picture of student life.

Curriculum, teaching and assessment

Of all the developments attempted by higher education institutions to improve the experience of ethnic minority students, transformation of the curriculum remains the area of least achievement. It is now an important priority to ensure that the curriculum, in particular in core subject areas, includes equal opportunity, black studies, religious and ethnic minority issues wherever possible.

This need for the reform of the central curriculum should not be confused with the desirability for black and ethnic studies options to be widely available. In this latter respect, a number of universities have made significant improvements in recent years.

It is important to note that this argument is not without its critics. For example, Coffield and Vignoles (1997) have expressed several reservations concerning moves to develop a multicultural curriculum in higher education. They argue that such measures could be 'culturally confirming' and that employers widely regard such courses as of low status. The first argument may be challenged by noting that current practice assumes and 'culturally confirms' a Eurocentric curriculum. A balanced multicultural curriculum can be developed which informs and raises issues without producing cultural stereotypes. Furthermore, if multiculturalism is seamlessly embedded in the curriculum (as Eurocentrism currently is), without changing the title of the award, employers could raise no legitimate objection. Indeed, the development of an international and multi-cultural curriculum may be seen to enhance graduates' employ-ability. This is perhaps a debate that has only just begun and it is worth reflecting on the survey findings in Chapter 8 that ethnic minority students are divided on the merits of a multicultural curriculum.

Much more research is needed to provide guidance on changes needed to teaching and learning strategies to support the needs of ethnic minority students. Initial findings suggest that students differ in the way in which they enjoy and respond to different learning situations. For example, a survey has found that, in contrast to white students, ethnic minority students tended to dislike seminar and tutorial situations (Adia, 1996).

Criticisms by some ethnic minority students, particularly Caribbean males, of the way in which work placements are used on business, engineering and applied science courses need to be addressed (see Chapter 6). Whilst there is currently little evidence to substantiate some students' claims about agency discrimination, it is nevertheless important for black students to feel confident in the placement application process. Following the publication of the National Committee of Inquiry into Higher Education (the Dearing Report, 1997), which recommended wider use of work placements, it would seem essential for institutions to review work placement procedures to ensure conformity to equal opportunity principles. There should certainly be a halt to the common practice of sending photographs to agencies responsible for selecting placement applicants, and serious consideration should be given to anonymised initial applications in order to protect those with non-European names from possible discrimination.

There is an urgent need to review and revise current assessment practices to ensure that they facilitate equality of opportunity for individuals from all ethnic groups. Research cited in this volume suggests that we need to ensure that opportunities for intended or unconscious racism are removed from the assessment process. Fairness and equity in the assessment process must be achieved and be seen to be evident by ethnic minority students to restore confidence.

A difficult problem to resolve is the emergent evidence that different ethnic groups might excel in different modes of assessment. For example, van Dyke (Chapter 9) found that Caribbeans tended to do well in course work, but fared rather badly compared to other groups in formal written examinations. Perhaps the practice pioneered in some universities represents a way forward. In these cases, students are provided with choices in assessment modes. Of course, such a solution poses serious challenges for course managers who have to guarantee equity and quality control in the assessment system. Such measures may also be unpopular with course managers at a time when there is growing concern over plagiarism and other forms of cheating. Indeed, some course teams increasingly rely on unseen written examinations because they believe (perhaps, mistakenly) that it is more difficult to cheat in examinations compared to course work. Where abandonment of examinations is considered unsuitable, considerably more support should be given to training students in examination techniques. Effective strategies should include greater use of objective criteria-based assessment and anonymous marking for examinations and course work.

Changes needed in student support and learning opportunities

A range of measures need to be considered in order to address the difficulties which ethnic minority students experience in higher education. It is important to ensure that they receive appropriate support from both academic and student services if they are to have the confidence to build a pleasant and rewarding student experience. This is a particularly challenging situation because, as Hogarth (1997) has shown, white students report having enjoyed their time at university and having received much easier access to academic and pastoral support compared to the experiences of ethnic minority graduates.

Appropriate support for ethnic minorities must begin in their first days on campus. As van Dyke indicates in Chapter 9, more use could be made of expanded induction programmes designed to ease the transition to higher education. There are already successful pioneering pre-course programmes for mature students, such as the four-week award-winning Gateway to Higher Education course at Southampton Institute (Acland and Comrie, 1997). Pre-courses of this kind aim to ease the transition to higher education and improve retention rates by reinforcing study skills and subject knowledge and by building confidence. General programmes of this kind could be easily modified to meet the needs of specific ethnic minority groups. These courses also function to develop self-support groups and reduce social anxieties based on the fear of being alone and isolated from those of the same background. It is important to note here that the development of self-support groups from the Gateway course led students to feel more secure to mix with others of different ages and cultural backgrounds. In other words, social mixing rather than segregation can develop from the security generated by pre-course learning experiences of this kind.

Of course, special support for ethnic minority students needs to continue beyond induction. Some institutions, particularly in the new university sector, provide study assistance centres to provide individual and group assistance for students experiencing difficulties with particular aspects of their learning programmes. Learning support is typically provided for computing, mathematics, present-ations, essay and report writing and examinations. It is clear from the analyses of van Dyke (Chapter 9) and Allen (Chapter 7) that the availability of such central support is particularly important for Caribbean students, especially those who require additional training in formal examination techniques. More controversially, Paul Allen argues that special support should be available for black students in recognition of the racist barriers they experience and their special learning needs.

Of course, support for study skill development addresses only part of the needs of ethnic minority students in higher education. Many students also have social and spiritual needs which need to be addressed if they are able to feel secure and confident in their higher education institution. For this reason, institutions need to ensure that ethnic minority students are provided with support for their social and religious interests. More facilities are needed, including provision for ethnic clubs and societies. Where a number of students have a special religious need, such as Muslim prayer rooms with single sex washing facilities, these should be provided.

Staffing issues

No discussion about race and higher education would be complete without addressing the common complaint that there are too few ethnic minority staff in higher education institutions, particularly in senior academic positions. This issue is not only important in itself, but it is also a significant influence upon the experiences and perceptions of ethnic minority students in higher education.

Singh's analysis (Chapter 11) represents a rare attempt in the UK to evaluate the position and experiences of ethnic minority staff in higher education. He demonstrates that official statistics reveal a complex picture of representation by different ethnic groups. In particular, Singh found that non-UK ethnic minorities were far better represented in universities than UK minorities. This, he believes, may be partly due to the importance of recruiting overseas academic researchers with significant reputations. When the overall pattern of full-time and part-time employment is reviewed, Singh claims that it reveals a picture of marginalisation of UK ethnic minority academic staff compared to their white counterparts.

Singh argues that some ethnic minority academic staff feel victimised or discriminated against within higher education institutions. He cites evidence from recent industrial tribunal rulings which found in favour of ethnic minority academics against their employers. This finding, coupled with evidence of marginalisation in employment, leads Singh to argue that much more is needed to improve the position of ethnic minority academic staff. Singh notes, with disappointment, that only one third of higher education institutions surveyed have developed an equal opportunities policy. Among measures needed to redress inequalities, Singh calls for policies to be developed which focus upon promoting awareness of racism, equality of treatment and effective ethnic monitoring.

Although it should be recognised that more research is needed in this area before firm conclusions should be drawn, there are a number of policy issues which should be addressed by higher education institutions. If institutions are genuinely committed to promoting equal opportunities they need to ensure that recruitment, selection and promotion are regularly monitored with centralised, clear guidelines. In addition, advertising at all levels should be appropriately targeted, including placing advertisements in ethnic minority magazines where appropriate.

There should also be appropriate staff development for all staff to broaden knowledge, challenge ethnic stereotypes and promote ethnic sensitivity training. Such an anti-racist staff development strategy is required for both academic and support staff in order to promote a safe and positive higher education experience for all students.

Whilst ethnic minority students often advocate the need for one non-white race officer or, alternatively, an equal opportunities officer (see Chapter 6), ethnic minority staff would also benefit from such a development. Where such a post exists, staff and students know immediately who they can consult in order to obtain advice and support. In increasingly large and complex organisations, it is particularly important for universities to adopt a 'one stop' approach to providing help and guidance on race and equality issues.

Implementing changes

Research has shown that, whilst progress has been made towards increasing the numbers of higher education students from the ethnic minorities, much more needs to be done to improve their experience in higher education institutions. Whilst all institutions declare a commitment to equal opportunity, it is difficult to envisage many voluntarily allocating funds to achieve significant improvements during a time of severe funding cutbacks. In particular, the provision of specialist facilities for religious and culturally distinct groups is unlikely to be high on the agenda of institutions who are struggling to maintain the quality of their overall student support services.

Major changes to support the needs of ethnic minority students will only be effective if responsibility for implementing change becomes a priority for the national bodies responsible for monitoring student statistics, conducting quality audits and the distribution of funding. Fortunately, the growing body of research evidence available in recent years has provided these bodies with the evidence which they needed to reevaluate their priorities and to attempt to address equal opportunities and race issues in a more direct manner.

It is therefore particularly encouraging to note that HEFCE and HEQC have made it clear that they will use their audit and evaluation powers to focus more attention upon the suitability of the curriculum, teaching and learning strategies and student support for the needs of ethnic minority students. It is also notable that HESA, which is responsible for compiling and analysing student statistics, is beginning to make more demands on institutions to provide detailed analysis of student progression, retention and achievement rates. It is hoped that such a high profile approach to these issues by such powerful national agencies will encourage institutions to radically reassess priorities and make appropriate changes to improve the equality of educational experience for all their students.

Finally, it is worth reflecting upon lessons which the UK can learn from other countries committed to widening participation for ethnic minorities. For example, according to Coffield and Vignoles (1997), the Australian practice of careful monitoring for the representation of non-traditional students and linking this to funding could be adopted in Britain. This would certainly logically follow from the recommendations of the Dearing Committee (1997) and it would function, in the short term, to redistribute funding towards new universities in metropolitan locations which are much favoured by ethnic minority students. In the longer term, this measure might have the benefit of encouraging the elite universities to reconsider recruitment policies, with obvious benefits for non-traditional student representation.

References

Acland, T and Comrie, A (1997) *Making the Transition to Higher Education –
What Motivates Adult Learners?* Paper delivered to SEDA Annual
Conference, Plymouth

Acland, T and Siriwardena, S (1989) 'Integration and segregation in an Asian
community', *New Community* 15 (4) 565–576

Adia, E (1996) *Higher Education: The Ethnic Minority Student Experience.*
Leeds: Heist

Aggleton, P and Whitty, G (1985) 'Rebels without a cause? Socialization and
subcultural style among the children of the new middle class'. *Sociology of
Education,* 58 (1), 60–72

Allen, R A (1992) 'The color of success: African-American college student
outcomes at predominantly white and historically black public colleges
and universities', *Harvard Educational Review* 62 (1) 26–44

Arora, R (1995) 'Experiences of ethnic minority students in higher
education'. In P Cohen (ed) op.cit.

Ballard, C and Ballard, R (1977) 'The Sikhs: The development of South Asian
settlements in Britain'. In J L Watson (ed) *Between Two Cultures.* Oxford:
Blackwell

Ballard, R and Holden, R (1975) 'The employment of coloured graduates in
Britain', *New Community* 4 (4) Autumn

Ballard, R and Vellins, S (1985) 'South Asian entrants to British universities:
A comparative note', *New Community,* 12 (2), 260–265

Banton, M (1988) *Racial Consciousness.* Essex: Longman

Basit, T N (1997) *Eastern Values, Western Milieu: Identities and Aspirations
of Adolescent British Muslim Girls.* Basingstoke: Ashgate

Bhachu, P (1985) *Twice Migrants.* London: Tavistock

Bird, J (1996) *Black Students and Higher Education: Rhetorics and Realities.*
Milton Keynes: Open University Press

Bird, J, Ching Yee W and Myler, A (1992a) *Widening Access to Higher
Education for Black People.* Bristol Polytechnic and Employment
Department

Bird J et al (1992b) *Ethnic Monitoring and Admission to Higher Education,*
Bristol Polytechnic/Employment Department

Bird, J et al (1992c) 'Rhetoric of access-realities of exclusion? Black students into higher education', *Journal of Access Studies* 7 (2), Autumn, 146–161

Bourdieu, P (1990) *In Other Words: Essays Towards a Reflexive Sociology.* Cambridge: Polity Press

Bourner, T and Hamed, M (1987) *Entry Qualifications and Degree Performance.* CNAA Development Service Pub. 11, London: CNAA

Brah, A (1992) 'Women of South Asian origin in Britain'. In P Braham, A Rattansi and R Skellington (eds) *Racism and Antiracism: Inequalities, Opportunities and Policies.* London: Sage, 64–78

Brah, A and Minhas, R (1985) 'Structural racism or cultural difference'. In G Weiner (ed) *Just a Bunch of Girls.* Milton Keynes: Open University Press, 14–25

Brah, A and Shaw, S (1992) *Working Choices.* London: Department of Employment

Breinburg, P (1987) 'The black perspective in higher education: A question of conflicting views', *Multicultural Teaching* 1 (6), Winter, 36–37

Brennan, J and McGeevor, P (1987) *Employment of Graduates from Ethnic Minorities.* London: Commission For Racial Equality

Brennan, J and McGeevor, P (1990) *Ethnic Minorities and the Graduate Labour Market.* London: Commission for Racial Equality

Carby, H (1982) 'Schooling in Babylon', *The Empire Strikes Back.* Centre for Contemporary Cultural Studies. London: Hutchinson

Casey, K (1993) *I Answer with My Life: Life Histories of Women Teachers Working for Social Change.* New York: Routledge

Clarke, S (1988) 'Another look at the degree results of men and women', *Studies in Higher Education* 13 (3) 315–331

Coffield, F and Vignoles, A (1997) *Widening Participation in Higher Education by Ethnic Minorities, Women and Alternative Students.* Report No 5. The National Committee of Inquiry into Higher Education

Cohen, P (1995) *For A Multicultural University.* Working Paper 3. London: New Ethnicities Unit, University of East London

Cohen, P (1995) 'The crisis of the western university'. In P Cohen (ed) op. cit.

Collier, J and Burke, A (1986) 'Racial and sexual discrimination in the selection of medical students for London medical schools', *Medical Education* 20, 86–90

Collins, P (1991) *Black Feminist Thought: Knowledge Consciousness and the Politics of Empowerment.* London: Routledge

Commission For Racial Equality (1991) *Commissioners' Items.* Notes of speeches made by the Deputy Chairman, Mr Ramindar Singh, at conferences at Bradford University, 10–11 July and Sheffield City Polytechnic, 6 July. Unpublished

Commission for Racial Equality (1992) *Ethnic Monitoring in Education.* London: CRE

Commission for Racial Equality (1996) *Report of a Formal Investigation: Appointing NHS Consultants and Senior Registrars.* London: Commission for Racial Equality

Commission on University Career Opportunity (1994) *A Report on Universities' Policies and Practices on Equal Opportunities in Employment.* London: CUCO

Connolly, P (1995) 'Racism, masculine peer-group relations and the schooling of African/Caribbean infant boys', *British Journal of Sociology of Education,* 16 (1), 75–92

Cooper, P, Upton, G and Smith, C (1991) 'Ethnic minority and gender distribution among staff and pupils in facilities for pupils with emotional and behavioural difficulties', *British Journal of Sociology of Education,* 12 (1), 77–94

Crace, J (1995) 'Urging greater expectations', *The Education Guardian,* 13 January

CRE/EOC/CVCP (1997) *Higher Education and Equality: A Guide.* Manchester: Equal Opportunities Commission

Department for Education (1992) *Exclusions: A Discussion Document.* London: DFE

Department for Education and Employment (1997) *Permanent Exclusions from Schools in England 1995/96.* London: DfEE

Drew, D (1995) *'Race', Education and Work: The Statistics of Inequality.* Basingstoke: Avebury

Drew, D, Gray, J and Sime, N (1992) *Against the Odds: The Education and Labour Market Experiences of Black Young People.* Youth Cohort Study of England and Wales, Research & Development Report No. 68. Sheffield: Employment Department

Driver, G (1979) 'Classroom stress and school achievement: West Indian adolescents and their teachers'. In V Saifullah Khan (ed) *Minority Families in Britain: Support and Stress.* London: Macmillan, 131–44

Edwards, R (1990) 'Access and assets: The experience of mature mother-students in higher education', *Journal of Access Studies* 2 (5) Autumn, 188–203

Employment Gazette (1993) 'Ethnic origins and the labour market'. Employment Department, February, London: HMSO

Employment Gazette (1995) 'Ethnic minorities'. Employment Department, June. London: HMSO

Epstein, D (1993) *Changing Classroom Cultures.* Stoke-on-Trent: Trentham

Equal Opportunities Review (1995) *Discrimination Case Law Digest* 25, 2–3

Esmail, A and Carnall, D (1997) 'Tackling racism in the NHS', *British Medical Journal* 314, 618–619

Esmail, A and Everington, S (1993) 'Racial discrimination against doctors from ethnic minorities', *British Medical Journal* 306, 691–692

Esmail, A and Everington, S (1994) 'Complaints may reflect racism', *British Medical Journal* 308, 1374

Esmail, A and Everington, S (1997) 'Asian doctors are still being discriminated against', *British Medical Journal* 314, 1619

Esmail, A, Nelson, P and Everington, S (1996) 'Ethnic differences in applications to United Kingdom medical schools between 1990–1992', *New Community* 22 (3) 495–506

Esmail, A, Nelson, P, Primarolo, D and Toma, T (1994) 'Applications to medical school: Is there racial discrimination?' *British Medical Journal* 310, 501–502

Foster, P (1990) *Policy and Practice in Multicultural and Anti-Racist Education.* London: Routledge

Fuller, M (1980) Black girls in a London comprehensive school. In M Hammersley and P Woods (eds) *Life in School: The Sociology of Pupil Culture.* Milton Keynes: Open University Press, 77–88

Gallagher, A, Richards, N and Locke, M (1993) *Mature Students in Higher Education: How Institutions Can Learn From Experience.* London: Centre for Institutional Studies, University of East London

Gibson, M A and Bhachu, P K (1988) 'Ethnicity and school performance: A comparative study of South Asian pupils in Britain and America', *Ethnic and Racial Studies,* 11 (3), 239–262

Gillborn, D (1990) *'Race', Ethnicity and Education: Teaching and Learning in Multi-Ethnic Schools.* London: Routledge

Gillborn, D (1992) 'Racial violence and harassment'. In D Tattum (ed) *Understanding and Managing Bullying.* London: Heinemann, 161–172

Gillborn, D (1996) *Exclusions from School.* Viewpoint No. 5. London: University of London Institute of Education

Gillborn, D and Gipps, C (1996) *Recent Research on the Achievements of Ethnic Minority Pupils.* London: Office for Standards in Education/HMSO

Gilroy, P (1987) *There Ain't No Black in the Union Jack.* London: Hutchinson

GMB (1993) *Divided by Degrees.* London: General, Municipal and Boiler-makers' Union

Gore, C (1996) *The Relationship Between 'School Effectiveness' and the Achievement of Pupils of Different Ethnic Origins.* Paper presented to Racism and Welfare Conference, University of Central Lancashire, 2 April 1996

Hagell, A and Shaw, C (1996) *Opportunity and Disadvantage at Age 16.* London: Policy Studies Institute

Hall, S (1992) 'New ethnicities'. In J Donald and A Rattansi (eds) *'Race', Culture and Difference*. London: Sage, 252–259

Higher Education Council for England (1996a) *Widening Access to Higher Education*. Bristol: HEFC

Higher Education Council for England (1996b) *Assessors' Handbook*. Bristol: HEFCE

Higher Education Statistic Agency (1995) *Students in Higher Education Institutions*. Bristol: HESA

Higher Education Statistic Agency (1996) *Resources of Higher Education Institutions 1994/5*. Cheltenham: HESA

HEQC (1996) *Learning from the Second Audit*. London: HMSO

Hogarth, T (1997) *The Participation of Non-traditional Students in Higher Education*. HEFCE Research Series. Institute of Employment Research

hooks, b (1991) *Yearning: Race, Gender and Cultural Politics*. London: Turnaround

hooks, b (1994) *Teaching to Transgress: Education and the Practice of Freedom*. London: Routledge

Housee, S, Williams, J and Willis, P (1990) 'Access to what? Black students' views of their higher education experiences', *Journal of Access Studies* 5 (2), Autumn, 203–213

ILEA Afro-Caribbean Language and Literacy Project (1990) *Language and Power*. London: Harcourt, Brace and Javanovitch

ILEA Language and Literacy Unit (1989) *Aspect of Language Across the College*. London: ILEA

Jenkins, R (1986) *Racism and Recruitment: Managers, Organisations and Equal Opportunity in the Labour-Market*. Cambridge: Cambridge University Press

Jewson, N et al (1991) 'Universities and ethnic minorities: The public face', *New Community* 17 (2) 183–199

Johnson, R (1988) 'Really useful knowledge 1790–1850: Memories for education in the 1980s'. In T Lovett (ed) *Radical Approaches to Education: A Reader*. New York: Routledge

Jones, T (1993) *Britain's Ethnic Minorities*. London: Policy Studies Institute

Keith, M (1993) *Race, Riots and Policing: Lore and Disorder in a Multiracist Society*. London: UCL Press

Keith, M (1995) 'Shouts of the street: Identity and spaces of authenticity', *Social Identities* 1 (2), 297–315

Kobrak, P (1992) 'Black student retention in predominantly white regional universities: The politics of faculty involvement', *Journal of Negro Education* 61 (4) 509–530

Krueger (1994) *Focus Groups*, 2nd ed. London: Sage

Lang, M and Ford, C (eds) (1988) *Black Student Retention in Higher Education.* Springfield, Ill.: Charles C Thomas Pub.

Langridge, A (1993) 'The performance of access students in higher education', *Journal of Access Studies* 8 (2) 255–260

Luttrell, W (1992) 'Working class women's ways of knowing: Effects of gender, race and class'. In J Wrigley (ed) *Education and Gender Equality.* London: Falmer Press

Mac an Ghaill, M (1988) *Young, Gifted and Black.* Milton Keynes: Open University Press

Mac an Ghaill, M (1989) 'Coming-of-age in 1980s England', *British Journal of Sociology of Education,* 10 (3), 273–86

Mac an Ghaill, M (1994) *The Making of Men: Masculinities, Sexualities and Schooling.* Buckingham: Open University Press

McCarthy, C (1990) *Race and Curriculum.* Lewes: Falmer

McCarthy, C and Apple, M W (1988) 'Race, class, and gender in American educational research: toward a nonsynchronous parallelist position', in L Weis (ed) *Class, Race, and Gender in American Education.* New York: State University of New York Press

McCrum, N G (1994) 'The academic gender deficit at Oxford and Cambridge', *Oxford Review of Education* 20 (1) 3–26

McLaren, P (1994) 'Multiculturalism and the postmodern critique: towards a pedagogy of resistance and transformation'. In H Giroux and P McLaren (eds) *Between the Borders: Pedagogy and the Politics of Cultural Change.* London: Routledge

McManus, I C, Richards, P and Maitlis, S L (1989) 'Prospective study of the disadvantage of people from ethnic minority groups applying to medical schools in the United Kingdom', *British Medical Journal* 298, 723–726

Middleton, B J (1983) *Factors Affecting the Performance of West Indian Boys in a Secondary School.* Unpublished MA Thesis, University of York

Mirza, H S (1992) *Young, Female and Black.* London: Routledge

Mirza, H S (1994) 'Making sense of the black female student experience in higher education', Paper given at the Society for Research in Higher Education (SRHE) conference, *The Student Experience.* University of York, December

Mirza, H S (1995) 'Black women in higher education: Defining a space/finding a place'. In L Morley and V Walsh (eds) *Feminist Academics: Creative Agents For Change.* London: Taylor & Francis

Mirza, H S (1997) 'Black women in education: A collective movement for social change', in H S Mirza (ed) *Black British Feminism: A Reader.* London: Routledge

Mirza, H S (1998) 'Race, gender and IQ: the social consequence of a pseudoscientific discourse', *Race Ethnicity and Education* 1 (1)

Mohanty, C T (1994) 'On race and voice. Challenges for liberal education in the 1990s', in H A Giroux and P Mclaren (eds) *Between Borders*. London: Routledge

Modood, T (1990) 'Catching up with Jesse Jackson: Being oppressed and being somebody', *New Community* 17 (1), 87–98

Modood, T (1992) 'Political blackness and British Asians', *Sociology* (28) 3

Modood, T (1993) 'The number of ethnic minority students in British higher education', *Oxford Review of Education* 19 (2), 167–182

Modood, T (1997) ' "Difference", cultural-racism and anti-racism'. In P Werbner and T Modood (eds) *Debating Cultural Hybridities: Identities and the Politics of Anti-Racism*. London: Zed Books

Modood, T, Beishon, S and Virdee, S (1994) *Changing Ethnic Identities*. London: Policy Studies Institute

Modood, T, Berthoud, R, Lakey, J, Nazroo, J, Smith, P, Virdee, S and Beishon, S (1997) *Ethnic Minorities in Britain: Diversity and Disadvantage*. London: Policy Studies Institute

Modood, T and Shiner, M (1994) *Ethnic Minorities and Higher Education: Why Are There Differential Rates of Entry?* London: Policy Studies Institute

Moore, R (1996) 'Back to the future: The problem of change and the possibilities for advance in the sociology of education', *British Journal of Sociology of Education*, 17 (2), June, 145–161

Moyo Robbins, M (1995) 'Black students in teacher education', *Multicultural Teaching* 14 (1), 15–22

NATFHE (1996) *Race Equality in Further and Higher Education*. London: National Association of Teachers in Further and Higher Education

National Committee of Inquiry into Higher Education (Dearing Committee) (1997) London: HMSO

Neophytou, E M, Chan, S M and East, P (1995) 'Encouraging access: Language across the ITT Curriculum'. In V Showunmi and D Constantine-Simms (eds) *Teachers for the Future*. England: Trentham Books

Neophytou, E M, East, P and Chan, S M (1996) ' Enhancing the educational experience of bilingual students on Initial Teacher Training courses', *Multicultural Teaching*, 15 (1), 29–33

Nettles, M T (ed) (1988) *Toward Black Undergraduate Student Equality in American Higher Education*. Westport, Conn.: Greenwood Press Inc.

NHSE (1997) *Hospital Medical Staff – England and Wales – National and Regional Tables. 1997*. London: Statistics (workforce) Branch. Department of Health, NHSE

Office for Standards in Education (1995) *The OFSTED Handbook*. London: HMSO

Office of Minority Affairs (1991) *Diversity Directory*. Ann Arbor: University of Michigan

Omi, M and Winant, H (1994) *Racial Formation in the United States*. New York: Routledge

Owen, D (1993) *Ethnic Minorities in Great Britain: Economic Circumstances*, 1991 Census Statistical Paper No 3. Warwick: University of Warwick

Owen, C, Mortimore, P and Phoenix, A (1997) 'Higher educational qualifications'. In V Karn (ed) *Ethnicity in the 1991 Census, Vol. 4: Employment, Education and Housing Among Ethnic Minorities in Britain*. London: OPCS

Page, T, Pearce, G, Pearl, L and Tam, C (1994) *An Analysis of Student Performance by Age, Gender, Entry Qualifications and Ethnic Group*. Paper presented at SHRE Conference, December 1994

Rahme, I A (1995) 'How do you rate in the "Impartial Career Guidance Stakes"?' *Careers Guidance Today*

Rattansi, A (1992) 'Changing the subject?' In J Donald and A Rattansi (eds) *'Race, Culture and Difference*. London: Sage, 11–48

Reay, D (1998) *Class Work: Mothers' Involvement in their Children's Primary Schooling*. London: Taylor and Francis

Reay D and Mirza, H S (1997) 'Uncovering genealogies of the margin: Black supplementary schooling', *British Journal of Sociology of Education*, 18 (4), December, 477–499

Robson, M (1987) *Language, Learning and Race*. London: Longman and FEU

Rose, H (1991) 'Case studies'. In G Allan and C Skinner (eds) *Handbook for Research Students in the Social Sciences*. Lewes: Falmer Press

Rosen, V (1990) *Beyond Higher Education*. London: North and East London Open College Network

Sargeant, R and Walker, G (1992) *Black Staff and F/HE Institutions: A note towards the realisation of equal opportunities within the academic workforce*. Paper given to the Cross Borough Equal Opportunities Group, Wolverhampton

Sewell, T (1995) 'A phallic sesponse to schooling: black masculinity and race in an inner-city comprehensive'. In M Griffiths and B Troyna (eds) *Antiracism, Culture and Social Justice in Education*. Stoke-on-Trent: Trentham, 21–41

Sewell, T (1997) *Black Masculinities and Schooling: How Black Boys Survive Modern Schooling*. Stoke-on-Trent: Trentham

Shepherd, D (1987) 'The accomplishment of divergence', *British Journal of Sociology of Education*, 8 (3), 263–76

Skellington, R with Morris, P (1992) *'Race' in Britain Today*. London: Sage

Singh, R (1990) 'Ethnic minority experience in higher education', *Higher Education Quarterly*, 44 (4), Autumn, 344–359

Siraj-Batchford, I. (1990) 'Access to what? Black students' perceptions of initial teacher education', *Journal of Access Studies* 2 (5) Autumn, 177–187

Siraj-Blatchford, I (1991) 'A study of black students' perceptions of racism in initial teacher education', *British Educational Research Journal* (17) 1, 35–50

Smith, D J and Tomlinson, S (1989) *The School Effect: A Study of Multi-Racial Comprehensives.* London: Policy Studies Institute

Solomos, J (1988) *Black Youth, Racism and the State.* Cambridge: Cambridge University Press

Solomos, J (1989) *Race and Racism in Contemporary Britain.* London: Macmillan

Solomos, J and Back, L (1995) *Race, Politics and Social Change.* London: Routledge

Solomos, J and Back, L (1996) *Racism and Society.* London: Macmillan

Solomos, J and Singh, G (1990) 'Race equality, housing and the local state'. In W Ball and J Solomos (eds) *Race and Local Politics.* London: Macmillan

Steady, F C (1993) 'Women and collective action: Female models in transition'. In S M James and A P Busia (eds) *Theorizing Black Feminisms: The Visionary Pragmatism of Black Women.* London: Routledge

Swann, Lord (1985) *Education for All: Final Report of the Committee of Inquiry into the Education of Children from Ethnic Minority Groups.* Cmnd 9453. London: HMSO

Taylor, P (1992a) *Ethnic Group Data for University Entry,* Project Report for CVCP Working Group on Ethnic Data. Warwick: Universty of Warwick

Taylor, P (1992b) 'Access to higher education: An uneven path?' In H Goulbourne and P Lewis-Weeks (eds) *Access of Ethnic Minorities to Higher Education.* Warwick: Centre for Research in Ethnic Relations, University of Warwick

Taylor, P (1992c) 'Ethnic group data and applications to higher education', *Higher Education Quarterly,* 46 (4)

Tomlinson, S (1981) *Educational Subnormality: A Study in Decision-Making.* London: Routledge and Kegan Paul

Tomlinson, S (1992) 'Disadvantaging the disadvantaged', *British Journal of Sociology of Education,* 13 (4), 437–46

Troyna, B and Carrington, B (1990) *Education, Racism and Reform.* London: Routledge

Troyna, B and Hatcher, R (1992) *Racism in Children's Lives.* London: Routledge

Twitchin, J (1995) 'Staff development in multicultural practice'. In P Cohen (ed) op.cit.

Wagner, L (1996) *Widening Access to HE,* Paper given to 'Transforming Higher Education' conference, Leeds University

Van Dijk, T A (1991) *Racism and the Press*. London: Routledge

Vellins, S (1985) 'South Asian students in British universities: A statistical note', *New Community* 10 (2), 206–212

West, C (1990) 'The new cultural politics of difference'. In R Ferguson, M Gever, T Minh-ha and C West (eds) *Out There: Marginalisation and Contemporary Cultures*. New York: New Museum of Contemporary Art

Williams, J, Cocking, J and Davies, L (1989) *Words or Deeds. A Review of Equal Opportunities Policies in Higher Education*. London: Commission for Racial Equality

Wrench, J and Qureshi, T (1996) *Higher Horizons: A Qualitative Study of Young Men of Bangladeshi Origin*, Research Study 30 London: Department for Education and Employment

Wright, C (1986) 'School processes – an ethnographic study'. In J Eggleston, D Dunn and M Anjali (eds) *Education for Some: The Educational and Vocational Experiences of 15–18 year old Members of Minority Ethnic Groups*. Stoke-on-Trent: Trentham

Wright, C (1992) *Race Relations in the Primary School*. London: David Fulton Publishers

Young, I M (1990) 'The ideal of community and the politics of difference'. In L Nicholson (ed) *Feminism/Postmodernism*. London: Routledge

Yuval-Davis, N (1994) 'Women, ethnicity and empowerment'. In K Bhavnani and A Phoenix (eds) *Shifting Identities, Shifting Racisms*. London: Sage